ADORNING THE DARK

ANDREW PETERSON

ADORNING THE DARK

Thoughts on Community, Calling, and the Mystery of Making

PUBLISHING
BRENTWOOD, TENNESSEE

Published by B&H Publishing Group
Nashville, Tennessee

Dewey Decimal Classification: 234.13
Subject Heading: CREATIVE WRITING / CREATION (LITERARY,
ARTISTIC, ETC.) / SPIRITUAL GIFTS

Scripture references are taken from the English Standard
Version. ESV® Text Edition: 2016. Copyright © 2001 by Crossway
Bibles, a publishing ministry of Good News Publishers.

Cover design and illustration by Stephen Crotts.

6 7 8 9 10 11 12 • 28 27 26 25 24

For Christie Bragg

Without your tireless, faithful, encouraging, boots-on-the-ground work, most of the stuff in this book wouldn't have happened. Ideas are a breeze. Incarnating them is more like a hurricane, and you've ridden the storm with me and mine for twenty years now.

I can't thank you enough.

CONTENTS

PREFACE

Over the years I've been asked to teach about songwriting, novel writing, creativity and the arts, and community. Sometimes it's for a conference. Sometimes it's for a school, college, or seminary—and every time I feel out of my league. Part of that is due to the fact that I know what a knucklehead I am. Part of it is because I'm a practitioner, not an academic. That means I haven't hunkered over ancient tomes in a library researching the arts; nor have I written lengthy papers on the subject under the tutelage of a professor. It means I've learned by doing, which is a nice way of saying that I learned by doing it wrong half the time.

I was nineteen when I had a head-on collision with Jesus through the music of Rich Mullins, and I gave the next twenty-six to a stumbling pursuit of a calling. (If you can add, now you know how old I am.) That calling, as I understand it, is to use whatever gifts I've been given to tell the truth as beautifully as I can. I've written a few hundred songs, played a few thousand concerts, written a handful of books, and executive produced an animated short film based on those books. Somewhere along the way I realized the writing life (and life in general) works best in the confines of a community, which led to the creation of a ministry called The Rabbit Room.

The Rabbit Room, inspired in part by the Oxford Inklings, is a gathering point for Christians with a similar calling to try and tell the truth beautifully—and part of the point is that none of us can do it alone. There's no doubt in my mind that what's shaped me and my work more than any particular talent on my part has been living out a calling in the midst of a Christ-centered community.

I don't have a PhD (I'm holding out for an honorary doctorate, thank you), and for that matter, I wasn't a very good student. This teaching thing, then, is not something I foresaw. There are days when I dream about going back to school to really dig in, to be the old guy who sits on the front row and asks all the annoying questions, but then I talk to graduate students about the papers they're writing, the research involved, the defense of their theses—and I doubt that I have it in me to do something so rigorous. As you'll see, I've spent a lot of my life following my nose, usually turning up that nose whenever I'm expected to do something I don't feel like doing. I realize this is a weakness. But it's a weakness God has redeemed again and again, one that has gotten me into a lot of trouble, the getting out of which has always led to something healing or edifying.

I'm not afraid of hard work, but I do have an aversion to work that feels like a waste of time. That means I tend to throw myself into big projects, usually a few at a time, work until my mind is jelly, and if I don't have a proper break then I'm going to have a proper breakdown.

Many, many times over the years I've told my sweet Jamie, "We just have to make it until _____, then things will calm down, I promise," and there's some truth to it. But Jamie and I both know that once things calm down, some new harebrained idea will float to the surface of my gray matter and will start it all up again. My longsuffering manager Christie has the task of talking me out of truly dumb ideas, talking me into things I don't at first see the value in, coming up with a plan for the ideas that stick, and reminding me six months later when I'm frustrated and tired that this is exactly what I wanted to do—that it was *my* idea, after all.

To not learn at least *something* of value over the last few decades of creative work would be odd, and though I don't often feel very smart, I do in fact have some strong opinions about the way things are, and those opinions are based at least in part on experience.

The first few times I was in a position of leadership at a retreat or conference I was so nervous I could hardly speak. When my dear friend Kenny Woodhull asked me to co-lead a retreat with Michael Card about fifteen years ago, I declined. Putting on a concert is one thing; I could do that. But teaching? Speaking? Leading? Clearly Kenny had the wrong guy. But he talked me into it. At the first session of that retreat, after Michael gave his brilliant introductory thoughts, it was my turn to say a few words. I stammered as I told them that I felt unqualified, but that I had to trust something George MacDonald once wrote about the inner chamber of God's heart:

> As the fir-tree lifts up itself with a far different need from the need of the palm-tree, so does each man stand before God, and lift up a different humanity to the common Father. And for each God has a different response. With every man he has a secret—the secret of the new name. In every man there is a loneliness,

*an inner chamber of peculiar life into which God only
can enter . . . a chamber into which no brother, nay,
no sister can come.*

*From this it follows that there is a chamber also—
(O God, humble and accept my speech)—a chamber
in God himself, into which none can enter but the
one, the individual, the peculiar man—out of which
chamber that man has to bring revelation and strength
for his brethren. This is that for which he was made—to
reveal the secret things of the Father.*[1]

That is to say, you know and understand things about
the heart of God that only *you* can teach. Once I was in a
counseling session with my dear friend Al Andrews, working
through a painful season of my childhood. "I don't know
what's wrong with me," I said with a sniffle. "My brother and
sisters don't seem to carry this same pain, and we were all
there at the same time, in the same house." Al said, "If I were
to interview four siblings about their childhoods, they would
each describe a completely different family." Your story, then,
is yours and no one else's. Each sunset is different, depending
on where you stand. So when the voices in my head tell me I
have nothing to offer, nothing interesting to say, I fight back
with George MacDonald.

Jesus said, "In my Father's house are many rooms" (John
14:2). Could it be that those rooms are inner chambers in the

---

1. C. S. Lewis, *George MacDonald: An Anthology 365 Readings*, "The New
Name" (Nashville, TN: HarperCollins, 2015).

heart of God, each of which has an individual's name on it? If this is true, and I'd like to believe it is, then all I have to do is tell about my Lord and my God. Because I know him intimately, uniquely, it may be a revelation, in a sense, of the secret things of the Father. This is part of my calling—to make known the heart of God. And because he holds a special place in his heart for me and me alone (just as he holds a special place for you), my story stands a chance to be edifying to my sisters and brothers, just as your story, your insight, your revelation of God's heart, is something the rest of us need.

In that spirit, this book is a glimpse into my own faltering journey as a songwriter, storyteller, and Christian. It's a love song, if you will, about the life God has given me.

BACH'S SECRET WEAPON

I recently had a good, long phone conversation with a singer-songwriter about that grand old subject, Getting Started in the Music Business. He's recorded an album but hasn't yet taken the leap into full-time music and was asking me for some advice on the matter.

The problem is, I don't know what kind of practical career advice to give, because what worked in my case might not (and probably won't) work for you. I loved a pretty girl in college. I also loved to make music. I was freaking out because I thought I had to choose between her and the songs, until late one night my old friend Adam said, "If God wants you to play music, dummy, you'll play music whether you're married or not." So I married the girl.

You don't need a record contract to serve God with your gifts. You don't need to move to Nashville. You just need to stay where you are, play wherever you can, and keep your eyes peeled. You never know what might happen. One of the most fortuitous meetings in my life (my old buddy Gabe Scott) happened because I said yes to a 3:00 a.m., $40 gig at a junior high all-nighter. Gabe and I have been making music together now for more than twenty years.

But in the end, what did I do? I moved to Nashville. I got a record contract. It wasn't because I was some wildly successful indie bard, but because one guy heard my songs and believed in them enough to let me open for his band. What on earth do I know? The doors open. Walk through them.

The best thing you can do is to keep your nose to the grindstone, to remember that it takes a lot of work to hone your gift into something useful, and that you have to learn to enjoy the work—especially the parts you don't enjoy. Maybe *that's* the answer to a successful career. But I know far too many hard-working, gifted singer-songwriters or authors who work their fingers to the bone and still have to moonlight at a restaurant to make ends meet. Every waiter and waitress in Nashville has a demo in their back pocket, just in case. Me, I waited tables at Olive Garden for three months before suddenly finding myself on a tour bus wondering how in the world *that* happened.

So do you wait tables? Sure. Do you make the demo CD? Maybe, but don't bother carrying it around. Do you work hard at your craft? Definitely. Do you move? Quit your day job? Marry the girl? Borrow the start-up funds? Sign the deal?

Here's what I know in a nutshell: "Seek first the kingdom of God and his righteousness, and all these things will be added to you" (Matt. 6:33). Early on, I didn't always seek God's Kingdom first, and Lord knows his righteousness was only on my mind for a minute or two a day max (I think I'm up to three, maybe four minutes now). That simple Scripture draws into sharp focus the only thing that will satisfy us in our desperate seeking for what it is that we think we want. We may want something harmless, but if it's out of place, if it comes before the right thing, then what's benign becomes malignant. We want the wrong thing.

So boil it all down. Chop off the fat. Get rid of the pet lizard, because you can't afford to feed it anyway. Wrench your heart away from all the things you think you need for your supposed financial security, your social status. Set fire to your expectations, your rights, and even your dreams. When all that is gone, it will be clear that the only thing you ever really had was this wild and Holy Spirit that whirls about inside you, urging you to follow where his wind blows.

If you can put aside your worry long enough to feel that wind and to walk with it at your back, it will lead you to a good land. It will remind you that righteousness means more than pious obedience; it means letting a strong, humble mercy mark your path, even when—especially when—you don't know where it's taking you. It may not take you to an easy chair in a Nashville mansion with a Grammy on the mantel; it probably won't lead you to head-turning fame, and it probably won't even lead you to a feeling that you're a righteous, Kingdom-seeking saint. Because if that's what you are you'll probably *feel* more like a sinful, desperate cur who can get out of bed each day only because you've managed once again to believe that Christ's mercy is made new every time the sun ascends. You're a sinful, desperate cur who dances for joy. Your heart is so full it must be poured out. You see the world as a dark, messy place that needs rearranging, and with all that light shooting out of your pores you're just the person to do it.

See how the questions of career choices and demo CDs and relocating diminish in light of God's Kingdom?

Sail by the stars, not the flotsam.

———

I remember lying on my bed in high school with two cabinet speakers on either side of my head, listening to Pink Floyd's *A Momentary Lapse of Reason*, getting delightfully lost in the music and wondering how on earth this band of Brits transferred their music to two-inch tape, then to cassette, then to the record store, then to Lake Butler, Florida, to my speakers, to my ears, and finally to my adolescent noggin.

So with just a few chords under my fingers and a whole lot of ambition, not to mention the absence of enough guys in my little town to really start a band, I decided to try and figure out how to make music. I saved up four hundred bucks that I earned mowing yards and stocking shelves at the local IGA and bought a Tascam four-track recorder, a machine I was certain would revolutionize my life—not just musically but relationally, since now I would be able to prove to the girls in school that I was worth something. "You see," I imagined myself explaining to them, "I can record four separate tracks onto just *one* cassette, which allows me to play the bass, the guitar, the drums, and sing, then mix it all together for your listening pleasure, ladies," at which point their eyes would flutter and they would faint to the floor in a pile of crimped hair and leg warmers.

But that was just the recording gear. I also needed a studio. Enter my pal Wade Howell, also known as the Conundrum. He was a football player who was also a part-time atheist, a saxophonist, guitarist, and Dungeon & Dragons gamemaster. Needless to say, we were fast friends. (For the record, Wade ended up going to seminary and is now a pastor and a fine family man.) Our senior year of high school Wade's grandfather died and left him a single-wide trailer in the woods, where we set up an old drum kit and a few mics I scavenged from the church sound cabinet. After school, while Wade was at football practice, I often sped down the sandy road in my Dodge Omni to the trailer, plugged in Wade's electric guitar, and pretended I was David Gilmour or Tom Petty. Once, because my girlfriend liked Garth Brooks, I used my trusty Tascam to record the drums, piano, bass, and vocals for the song "The Dance." What I wouldn't give to know where that cassette is now.

But after the first few months with the Tascam, the magic was gone. I didn't want to just record Skynyrd songs. I wanted to make my own. But I had no idea what to sing about, and the few songs I managed to write were even worse than I thought they were at the time. I played them bashfully for my buddies, enjoying the feeling of having made something even though I was inwardly discontent. It strikes me now that I was in possession of an inner-critic even then, which agitated me. I wanted to be content with my lame songs, but I couldn't be. Whatever pride I felt was in having made something—anything at all—not necessarily in the quality of what had been made. So I shared my songs with the few friends who cared to hear them, and felt good when they liked them, but was discontent without knowing why. Not long after graduation, I joined a rock band and sold the Tascam, figuring that I'd leave recording to the experts and focus on rocking instead.

Fast-forward two years. The rocking was safely behind me. I was now in college, married, and taking serious steps with our band Planet X to record a demo. At the time, I had no idea there was such a thing as indy music. As far as we knew, the game plan was to record a demo and shop it around in Nashville. So Lou, the only guy in the band with any money, bought some gear, and we set out to record our stuff after-hours in the college practice rooms. It turned out fine enough, but it was a far cry from what it needed to be. Eventually the band broke up. I started doing my own concerts, and I realized I had enough of my own songs to record a short album. I borrowed $3,000 from my grandma, took a Greyhound to Nashville (just like they do in the movies), was picked up at the bus station by my old roommate Mark Claassen, and spent the weekend recording my independent record *Walk*.

It was terrifying, exhilarating, and exhausting. We were in a real studio. We hardly slept. We recorded, mixed, and mastered eight songs in 2.5 days. I took the Greyhound home (a grueling twenty-six hour trip, what with all the bus stops), a twenty-two-year-old kid with a shiny, $3,000 CD in his guitar case and not a dime to his name. We'd only been married for a year, but Jamie was all in, as she's always been. That little eight-song CD was what I sold at concerts for the next three years, and I'll be forever glad for the way it paid the rent. But the farther I got from it the more I loathed it. I became painfully embarrassed by my voice, my pitch, and my songs, because I had come to know better. I had toured with Caedmon's Call for fifty shows, which exposed me to some great music and a much better understanding of what it meant to be a songwriter. I was no longer doing the Florida church camp circuit, but was trying to make a go of a real career, and that meant I could no longer be content with my mediocre best. I had to work at it, learn to be objective, and—this is the big one—ask for help, help, help.

Which brings me to that day in East Nashville, fifteen years later, when I walked into Cason Cooley's studio, a warm room strung with lights and fragrant with incense, jammed full of guitars and pianos and books, and sat down with my friends to start a new project. I looked around, thinking about all the other times I had done this very thing, marveling at how little I still knew about it. What do we do first? Do we sit around and play the songs for a day? Do we record scratch guitars? Do we pore over lyrics first? In some ways, it's like looking at a hoarder's house and wondering where to begin the cleanup. It's also like looking out at a new field, steeling your resolve to tame it, furrow it, and plant—but you know it's littered with stones and it's going to be harder than you think.

I was a grown-up. This wasn't my first rodeo. I shouldn't have felt that old fear, anxiety, or self-doubt, right? Then again, maybe I should have. As soon as you think you know what you're doing, you're in big trouble. So before we opened a single guitar case, we talked. I sat with Ben Shive, Andy Gullahorn, and Cason and told them I felt awfully unprepared. I doubted the songs. I was nervous about the musical direction the record seemed to want to take. I wondered if I was up to the task. I told them about the theme that had arisen in many of the songs: loss of innocence, the grief of growing up, the ache for the coming Kingdom, the *sehnsucht*[2] I experience when

---

2. This is a word that will come up more than once in this book, so it's worth defining. C. S. Lewis described *sehnsucht* as "inconsolable longing," and even pointed to it as a proof for the existence of God. We all feel it. We're all familiar with it on some level. What's it there for if we're just meaningless clusters of cells hurtling through

I see my children on the cusp of the thousand joys and ten thousand heartaches of young-adulthood.

Then we prayed. We asked for *help*.

If you're familiar with Bach, you may know that at the bottom of his manuscripts, he wrote the initials, "S. D. G." *Soli Deo Gloria*, which means "glory to God alone." What you may not know is that at the top of his manuscripts he wrote, "Jesu Juva," which is Latin for "Jesus, help!" There's no better prayer for the beginning of an adventure. Jesus, you're the source of beauty: help us make something beautiful; Jesus, you're the Word that was with God in the beginning, the Word that made all creation: give us words and be with us in *this* beginning of *this* creation; Jesus, you're the light of the world: light our way into this mystery; Jesus, you love perfectly and with perfect humility: let this imperfect music bear your perfect love to every ear that hears it.

We said, "Amen," and opened our eyes, gazing out across the chasm between us and the completion of the project. Then I took a deep breath, opened the guitar case, and leapt.

----

a meaningless universe? Frederick Buechner, as far as I know, didn't use this word, but his writings describe it (and evoke it) time and again, and he consistently exhorts us to pay attention to it. Pay attention to the moments when we're crying without knowing why. It could be that the author of the great mystery of creation is whispering to you.

2

IN THE BEGINNING

This is how it begins.

You mumble a phrase. It's gibberish, but it suggests a melody. You've gotten melodies in your head before, but this one feels different, like it's made of something stronger and older. You notice this because you're able to repeat it, and you like it, and you sing it again and again, enough times that you pull out your phone and record it. As soon as you get it down, you forget about it and move on.

Skip ahead a few days. Now you have your guitar in your lap. Fear and self-doubt are taunting ghosts at either shoulder. You try to find some combination of chords that doesn't sound like everything else you've ever played, or everything everyone else has ever played. But after twenty minutes you're sick of yourself and your guitar and the weather and your lack of talent. Then with a thrill of hope you remember that voice-mail message you left yourself in the moment of mumbled inspiration. You listen to the voice mail, and you're disappointed. It's not terrible, but it's missing whatever magic it had before. With nothing else to do, you try and find the chords that the mumbling melody wants. You play it through on the guitar a few times in standard tuning, key of G—the same four chords you learned when you were in eighth grade. Then you capo it up and try it with a different voicing. You happen upon a little pull-off with your index finger, a slightly different way of playing the same old chord. That sparks a melody that suits the gibberish a little better, and like a dying man in the desert who discovers a cactus, you get just enough juice to keep crawling.

"O God," you pray, "I'm so small and the universe is so big. What can I possibly say? What can I add to this explosion of glory? My mind is slow and unsteady, my heart is twisted and tired, my hands are smudged with sin. I have nothing—*nothing*—to offer."

Write about that.

"What do you mean?"

Write about your smallness. Write about your sin, your heart, your inability to say anything worth saying. Watch what happens.

And so, with a deep breath, you strum the chords again, quieting the inner taunts, the self-mockery. And you sing something that feels somehow like an echo of the music and the murky waters you're wallowing in and the words you mumbled several days ago. Then, after hours and days of the same miserable slog, something happens that you cannot explain: you realize you have a song. Behold, there is something new under the sun.

Writing about writing is precarious. On one hand it could be terribly self-indulgent, while on the other it could be terribly boring—both of which are cardinal sins when it comes to the written word. I spent way too much money on books about writing before Reed Arvin, a record producer-turned-novelist, told me, "Trash all those books about writing. Just sit down and write the darn book." I didn't throw all the books away, but I did stop reading them. There are a few that did me some good, and even fewer that did more than offer up pointers on writing—they taught me to think about the creative act as a kind of worship, as a way to be human.

Since we were made to glorify God, worship happens when someone is doing exactly what he or she was made to do. I ask myself when I feel God's pleasure, in the Eric Liddell sense, and it happens—seldom, to be sure, but it happens—when I've just broken through to a song after hours of effort, days of thinking, months of circling the song like an airplane low on fuel, searching desperately for the runway. Then I feel my own pleasure, too, a runner's high, a rush of adrenaline. I literally tremble. There is no proper response but gratitude. The spark of the idea was hope; the work that led to the song was faith; the completion of the song leads to worship, because in that startling moment of clarity when the song exists in time and history and takes up narrative space in the story of the world—a space that had been empty, unwritten, unknown by all who are subject to time—then it is obvious (and humbling) that a great mystery is at play.

I hope it's clear that I'm not talking about the quality (or lack thereof) of the song itself. That's irrelevant. The point is, time is unfolding like a scroll, and we're letters on the parchment, helping to make up the words that tell the story. Each of us is a character, in both senses of the word. At times, characters become aware that they're part of a story, and that brings the realization that, first, there is an author, and second, they are not him.

This realization is good and proper, and leads into the courts of praise, if not the throne room itself.

I wish I were a contemplative like Merton. I wish I could order my thoughts and follow them to their ends. I wish I could track an idea to its logical or illogical conclusion the way C. S. Lewis did. But if there's one thing I've learned, it's that I can't learn without doing; I won't know the story until I write it down. As long as the idea stays in the conceptual realm it withers.

So, here. Let me sit for a while and follow a thought. Let's see what happens if I dedicate the next chapter to utter transparency, with the hope that it'll help you see that you're not alone. I'm going to let you in on what's going on in my head—right now, in real time.

The first thought that sprouts like a thorny weed: *Who do I think I am, anyway?*

3

SCARED AND SACRED

Immediately, my mind is crowded with voices that tell me to stop. They tell me I don't have time to dig in; I need to leave in forty-five minutes for an appointment (an appointment, ironically, to teach a songwriting class). I'm not intelligent enough, or academic enough, or witty enough to offer any insight into this process. I have nothing new to say. And yet, the mere exercise of forcing myself to keep typing has produced a few sentences, maybe even a paragraph. A book is made up of sentences and paragraphs, and one look at the bookstore shelves should be enough to tell anyone that quality of writing is no prerequisite for being published. The one prerequisite for publication that is undeniable, it seems to me, is that one must write sentences and paragraphs. Check that off the list.

The next obvious thought is that I don't know what comes next. Should I stop writing long enough to form an outline? Would that count as writing? I doubt it.

When it comes to fiction, the page is a playground. I can, more or less, go where I want, clamber around on whatever monkey bars I choose. But since this is a book about writing in the real world, I'm bound by fences. I must make these avenues of sentences walkable, enjoyable even, by you, dear reader, and if not enjoyable then at least useful, no? What use is a useless book? Self-expression as an end is a hellish game. No, I want you to *feel* something, to learn something, to know something in a way that you never knew before.

Another thought screams overhead like an F-18: *You have nothing to teach.*

Is that true?

I think of the last twenty-five or so years of writing and figure I should have something to say. *Something*, surely. And yet, when I hear real writers speak, I gobble their words like a hungry dog, wishing I were as wise as they are.

(Reminder: this isn't a pity party. I'm just letting you in on the grim reality of what goes on in a person's head when they do creative work, mainly so you'll know you're not crazy. Or alone.)

I carry a persistent fear that my thoughts are incorrect, or silly, or so obvious they aren't worth saying. Suddenly I'm a little boy, sitting in class like a solemn ghost. Mrs. Larson asks me a question, all the seven-year-old eyes in the room turn to me with expectation, and I'm frozen in place, terrified by the sudden realization that I'm expected to contribute. My cheeks flush and I want to go away to someplace safe—someplace like the woods or the eternal fields of green Illinois corn where I can watch and experience and listen without any demand to justify my existence. I've always been happy to be alone. God, however, never takes his eyes off me, and on my good days I believe that he is smiling, never demanding an answer other than the fact of myself. I exist as his redeemed creation, and that is, pleasantly, enough for him.

The rest of the world, though, is chugging along just fine whether I speak up or not. I'm the kid (and the man) who doesn't raise his hand. Whenever I do, I regret it. Better to keep quiet, to work out my rejection with fear and trembling, and to keep hunting for a safe place where I'm never confronted with my own insignificance. And yet, at war with that desire to be invisible is a yearning to be seen and known and valued. That's what really led to writing, if I'm honest. In the beginning it wasn't about glorifying my Maker—it was about declaring my own existence, for my own sake. It took a long time to realize that was a dead end. Literally. This book is about a better way, and even now I have to fight to follow it.

Being a writer doesn't just mean writing. It means *finishing*. I've heard it said that a song is never finished, only abandoned. That's not true for me. To the contrary, I can't wait to be done with the thing, because only once it's finished can I raise my hand at the back of the class and say something that will be considered, not ignored, something that might be a blessing to someone. Only then do I begin to take on some flesh and stop haunting the room. Walt Wangerin Jr. said once that art isn't art until it's experienced by another.

Praise God, I was reckless enough to try this thing—not because my songs matter all that much, but because I would have possibly gone mad—a madness of self-hatred, self-disdain, self-flagellation. A madness of Self. "Take thy thoughts captive," I imagine God saying. "Put them to music. Then aim them away from you. Love your neighbor as yourself." I confess, a mighty fear of irrelevance drove me to this vocation, a pressing anxiety that unless you looked back at me with a smile and a nod and said, "Oh, I see you. You exist. You are real to me and to this world and we're glad you showed up," I might just wither away and die. That's not exactly a noble reason to fling your creations into the world, but it's a decent place to start. After that, the Lord can redeem your impulse for self-preservation by easing you toward *love*, which is never about self. But if you're scared, there's no rush. First you have to *do* something. You have to climb out from under the bushel and share your light with those around you. You have to believe that you're precious to the King of Creation, and not just a waste of space.

You and I are anything but irrelevant. Don't let the Enemy tell you any different. We holy fools all bear God's image. We're walking temples of the Spirit, the bashful bride of Christ, living stones in what is going to be a grand house, as holy and precious as anything else in the universe, if not more so. God is making us into a Kingdom, a lovely, peaceful one, lit by his love for us flowing toward one another. That's the best gift you have to give.

––––––––––

A few miles from my house there's an intersection that used to make me happy. It's since been developed beyond recognition, and I regret to report that the magic is gone. If you ever want to go there, it's a four-way stop at the intersection of Old Franklin Road and Cane Ridge Road. It wasn't terribly interesting. It wasn't a scenic overlook. The houses weren't gigantic. But it was, for me, a strangely pleasant place. I don't know why, but I felt *rightness* every time I pulled up to that intersection. I'd always look around as if I were on the verge of solving some bright mystery—until the driver behind me honked and I was forced to putter up the hill.

I mentioned it to Jamie and the kids, and they agreed. It was a nice spot. To them, it was probably just that. But I would always wonder what made me feel that way. Was it the lie of the land? Was it the fact that the stop sign forced me to pause for a moment and consider my surroundings? Did it remind me of some lovely childhood drive? I can't put my finger on it.

Psalm 16:6 says, "The lines have fallen for me in pleasant places; indeed, I have a beautiful inheritance." I know the psalmist wasn't thinking of country roads when he wrote this, but I always thought of this verse when I sat at that intersection. "This, surely, is a pleasant place," I would say to myself. And in some ways, a pleasant place is better than a breathtaking one, isn't it? I love the Grand Canyon and have hiked into it a handful of times over the years, but I wouldn't want to live there.

Now, I realize, of course, that if Wendell Berry is right—that there are no unsacred places, only sacred places and desecrated places—then that intersection was just as sacred as the grass on your front lawn. But isn't it true that some places feel *right*, just as surely as other places feel wrong?

I have been to desecrated places, and have sensed a brooding darkness without knowing why. I have, at times, had to speak aloud what I believe to be true about God's presence in and around me in order to silence the voices of fear that clamored in my head—I have, in other words, been spooked. I have whistled in the dark. I don't know how all this works. I only know that we've all probably been in houses that felt dark and disquieting, and by contrast there's a sense of peace that seeps out of the walls of others. I want *my* house to be a house of peace. I want people to sense God's presence when they roll up our gravel driveway.

But how?

It's a matter of dedicating to God the world within our reach. Jamie and I are blessed with two wonderful neighbors, Tommy and Becky. When they built their home, sweet Becky wrote scripture verses on every 2 x 4 she could find. You can't see them anymore now that the house is finished, and of course they don't work as charms or anything weird like that; Bible verses on the studs don't do anything magical. Still, every sacred word that Becky wrote on every sacred plank of wood was a reminder to her that it was not *her* house, but God's.

The Christian's calling, in part, is to proclaim God's dominion in every corner of the world—in every corner of our hearts, too. It isn't that we're fighting a battle in which we must win ground from the forces of evil; the ground is already won. Satan is just an outlaw. And we have the pleasure of declaring God's Kingdom with love, service, and peace in our homes and communities. When you pray, dedicate your home, your yard, your bonus room and dishwasher and bicycle and garden to the King. As surely as you dedicate your heart to him, dedicate your front porch. Daily pledge every atom of every tool at your disposal to his good pleasure. It's all sacred anyway if old Wendell is right (and I think he is). I wonder if the Holy Spirit is rambling around in the temple of my heart, scribbling promises on every exposed bit of lumber, declaring my sacredness so that I will remember that I belong to him. And maybe when I'm old and I cross paths with some weary traveler, they'll sense a *rightness*, a pleasantness of place, and will experience a peace that they cannot understand or explain.

Stop a moment and look around. This is our Father's world. We are sacred, you and I.

And that's the answer to the question that ended chapter 2: *Who do I think I am, anyway?* We need not look anywhere but to the eyes of our Savior for our true identity, an identity which is profoundly complex, unfathomable, deep as the sea, and yet can be boiled down to one little word: *beloved.* That's it. And that's why it's so silly (and perilous) to use your gifting to clothe yourself with meaning. Those clothes will never quite fit.

I once heard someone suggest that in the new creation, the work of our hands will at last be equal to what we were able to imagine. But in the meantime, living as we do in dying bodies in a dying world, our best work always falls short of the initiating vision. Toil and trouble, thistle and thorn, we push through the brush and come out bloody on the other side, only to realize that we've ascended a false peak. It's difficult, yes. But it doesn't change a thing about *who* we are.

———

A few years ago I realized with a thud of dread that I had about a month to come up with the songs for a new album. I had two, maybe three ready to go, which meant I needed to write at least eight more songs, preferably ten or twelve. Some people start a record with forty or fifty in the queue and it's the producer's job to help the writer narrow them all down to the ten or twelve that will comprise the collection. Even when

I was in college, spending every spare minute writing because it helped me avoid schoolwork, I didn't have that many songs in the queue—ever. I'm so distrustful of my own abilities, my tendency is to abandon a song (or at least shelve it) as soon as I stop believing in it. It's possible, I suppose, that that method thwarts the output, never allowing a sloppy song the chance to grow into a good one, but after twenty years I might as well stick to what I know. So in a couple of months, six weeks, maybe, I knew I'd be in the studio with a producer, shaking hands with the drummer and bass player, teaching them the basic layout of a few songs. I should have felt some anxiety about it, but I didn't, mainly because there's a last-minute rush of creativity that accompanies every project, the way Jamie used to nest like a madwoman in the weeks before each of our children's births. (Never underestimate the power of a good panic to summon a song.)

One of them appeared while I was walking our woods. It arrived in the key of G, a 4/4 ballad that felt like something by British songwriter David Gray. I sang the first few words at the piano during a rare moment when Jamie and the kids were all out somewhere. (Never underestimate, either, the power of a quiet house, a few minutes in the half-light of late afternoon, when there's no fear of being overheard, when one can make a fool of oneself with abandon. King David may have danced through the streets of Jerusalem—but that's something I can't *imagine* doing, not for a million bucks.) I sang the first line, mumbled the rest, changed the chords underneath, and landed on a phrase that felt solid and meaningful, and at once I could imagine the dim shape of the finished work. A car pulled up the drive and the moment was gone, but I had a nibble—enough to tell me there were fish in the pond.

I walked around our home, over the stream by way of the wooden bridge that my son Asher built, up around the old dam and the empty pond, down to the pasture with the stone wall, thinking, thinking, thinking about what verse two might be. I started with the same few words of the first verse, then changed it up enough to suggest a parallel idea, and by the time I hiked past the statue of Saint Francis near the bend in the trail, there was another possible verse waiting to be sung at the piano—but not until I happened upon another miraculous moment of solitude when the house was empty.

At the risk of repeating myself, *this* is how it works. It's not magic. It's work. You think, you walk, you think some more, you look for moments to hammer it out on the piano, then you think again. A few days later I thrust the unfinished song upon Skye and Jamie, apologizing in advance for the discomfort such a performance would cause. That little performance is a crucial stage in the making of a song. You hear the song's weaknesses because you're able to listen to it through *their* ears. It's like taking your mom to a film you love, and only then realizing how offensive the language is. But it also exposes the song's strengths, if there are any. And this one, thank God, felt in the end like a proper song. A Song. An idea was introduced, a feeling conveyed, a response evoked. Weak and wobbly as its legs were, the thing took a few steps and held its ground. When the performance was over I ducked into my bedroom with a glimmer of hope.

Eight more to go. Eight more battles with fear. Eight more leaps of faith.

———————

Do you see how God redeemed, and continues to redeem, the broken and selfish motives that drove me here? How all those fears that bang around in my head are gathered, sifted like wheat, and then turned into something better than self-expression, self-preservation? I'll probably always be self-conscious, so the battle to make something out of nothing at all will rage on, and I'll have to fight it in the familiar territory of selfishness until the Spirit winnows my work into something loving and lovable. I'm no longer surprised by my capacity for self-doubt, but I've learned that the only way to victory is to lose myself, to surrender to sacredness—which is safer than insecurity. I have to accept the fact that I'm beloved by God. That's it. Compared to that, the songs don't matter so much—a realization which has the surprising consequence of making them easier to write.

4

BEHOLD THE LAMB

The Ryman Auditorium is a special place. Smack-dab in the middle of downtown Nashville, kneeling among all the honky-tonks and the neon lights and skyscrapers is a century-old red brick music venue that started out as a church, complete with stained glass windows and uncomfortable pews. It seats about two thousand people.

The first time I ever saw a show there was in 1995, when I drove up from Florida to see Rich Mullins on his *Brother's Keeper* tour. Ashley Cleveland and Carolyn Arends opened. I sat in the balcony—the best seats in the house, I know now—oblivious to the historic and spiritual significance of the place. Carolyn pulled out a camera between songs and said, "I can't believe I'm at the Ryman Auditorium. I have to document this." She took a picture of the audience, and everyone cheered—everyone but me, because I sat there wondering what the big deal was. Now I know better.

The Ryman stage has boasted legends like Johnny Cash, Hank Williams, Bob Dylan, Paul Simon, James Taylor, and Alison Krauss—but it will always be special to me because of a barefoot bard named Rich. Not just because the show was great, but because it was there that I snuck backstage and met him for the first time, and even though I made a total doofus of myself I'll always be thankful. Two years later, you see, Rich was dead. And two years later, I was living in Nashville.

Not long after moving to Music City, my buddy Gabe and I went to see Amy Grant do her big Christmas concert, not at the Ryman, but at the arena—a venue about two hundred times bigger and less intimate—and while I loved the concert (I really did), I remember thinking, "I think there's another way to do this." That was the night *Behold the Lamb of God* was born.

The idea struck and I couldn't ignore it: What if there was a Christmas concert that was only about Jesus? What if it told a story? And what if it didn't sound like your usual Christmas songs, but like the music I listened to the rest of the year? In other words, what if it sounded like Nashville, with dobros and hammered dulcimers and fiddles and folk singers, instead of Bing Crosby? Craziest of all, what if it happened at the Ryman?

High school Andrew would have been very surprised by all this. Back then I was way into rock and roll—everything from southern rock to hair metal. That may come as a surprise, given my folky vibe, but for years I listened to bands like Pink Floyd, Queensrÿche, Tesla, and Extreme. And each of those bands, in hindsight, had a direct influence on what was to become *Behold the Lamb of God*, because each of those bands released concept albums.

If you're under twenty you may be wondering two things: (1) Who are those bands you mentioned? and (2) What's a concept album? I won't bother with question number one, since there's this thing called the Internet. As for question two, the short answer is that a concept album is one that tells a story. Queensrÿche had a record called *Operation Mindcrime*, released when I was in eighth grade, which opened like a movie with a creepy voice saying, "I remember now. I remember how it started. I can't remember yesterday. I just remember doing . . . what they told me . . . told me . . . told me. . . ." And then

24

of course the band kicks in and takes us on a shredful journey complete with double-kick drum and a bunch of harmonized electric solos. As for me, I actually *don't* remember now . . . what the whole story of the album was . . . was . . . was. . . . I just remember that there was a storyline, however tenuous, that tied all the songs together. The same was true of Pink Floyd's *The Wall*, and Tesla's whole discography due to their obsession with Nikola Tesla, and especially Extreme's *Three Sides to Every Story*. The idea of an album in which all the songs are bound by a central idea intrigued me—especially when the connection wasn't obvious. Listening to the albums again and again was like trying to solve a puzzle; the story was just vague enough to keep me listening, hunting for clues.

With Extreme's *Three Sides*, though, it was a little more apparent. The concept of the album was the saying that there are three sides to every story: your side, my side, and the truth. The first part of the album (the "your" side) was three or four songs about war, politics, and the brokenness of the world. Side "me" included love songs, songs asking big questions about God. The third side had three songs that quoted Daniel and Jesus and ended with a magnificent Queen-like climax that tied together musical and lyrical themes from the rest of the record. Man, I listened to that album a zillion times. Incidentally, I played it for my current band a few months ago, and the whippersnappers pretty much hated it. I have to admit, it doesn't really hold up without the cultural context of what was going on in, uh, hair metal in the nineties. (I see you snickering.) But when I meet someone who connected to that record back in the day we always geek out.

The point is, all that stuff from high school is bubbling in the cauldron, and it floats to the surface in the most surprising ways. Even the stuff you're embarrassed about isn't beyond redemption.

In my case, I had to go to Bible College to complete the recipe that led to *Behold the Lamb*. My Old Testament professor always pointed out when Jesus showed up in the Hebrew Scriptures, whether in theme, theophany, prophecy, or foreshadowing. And though I'd grown up memorizing verses and listening to thousands of my dad's sermons, it wasn't until I was eighteen in that class that I realized Jesus is the center of it all. He holds the whole thing together. It was like God had written a concept album called the Bible, and I had finally realized what the story was. The story was *Jesus*. Everything clicked into place once I put him in the center. That's why, at the Amy Grant concert, I envisioned an album that hearkened back to Pink Floyd and Extreme but sounded like the kind of music I actually made, and most important, was about the Savior I had come to know. Not only that, I immediately thought of the Ryman. Wouldn't it be marvelous to sing those songs *there*, in the heart of this city I'd come to love?

I wrote "Gather 'Round, Ye Children, Come" back in early 2000 I think, and I told my manager Christie that I wanted to try a Christmas tour. No, I calmly explained, we wouldn't be singing traditional Christmas songs. Yes, the songs would tell a story. No, there wouldn't be speaking parts. No, the songs weren't written just yet, but seriously, how hard could it be?

No joke, we started booking shows before the songs were written.

Silers Bald was a great band with a terrible name. We randomly did a show together in Kansas in 2000, and when they covered Rich Mullins's "Calling Out Your Name," complete with a hammered dulcimer, I knew we'd be friends forever. At the time I was touring with just Gabe and Jamie (and our two babies, with my brother at the helm of the RV), and there was no way we could cover all the parts the Behold the Lamb instrumentation would demand. So I called the Silers guys and asked if they'd do the Christmas tour with us.

No, I calmly explained again, we wouldn't be doing traditional Christmas songs. No, there were no speaking parts, and so on. Amazingly, they said yes. In early December they made the trip to Nashville to rehearse. I still remember the looks of concern on their faces when we sat down to work out a show that wasn't quite like what anyone had ever done before. That concern turned to worry when I told them I was still writing some of the songs. But we set up in First Christian Church on Franklin Road (in a building since annexed by Franklin Road Academy, if you're keeping track) and got to work.

One of my clearest memories was of Randall Goodgame and my brother Pete showing up at the rehearsal to see what we were up to. After the first run-through they both told me we were on to something. Pete got choked up and said in an uncharacteristically tender way, "This is really special." I was scared, yes, but my fear was balanced out by my audacity. That flash of inspiration from the Amy Grant show was still burned into the retina of my inner eye, so no matter how incomplete the songs were we just had to play them. The first show, I think, was at Wellesley College, and I honestly have no idea why a prestigious all-girl school booked us at all. We all stood backstage, terrified of what was about to happen. It was rough. We messed up plenty. But I also have a distinct memory of the audience paying close attention, their faces stern while they listened, piecing together the story we were telling. The performance was far from perfect, but I think they could see what we were *trying* to do, and that was enough. Intention trumps execution—remember that. That's how the rest of the tour went. We weren't there yet, but we were on to something. I'll always be grateful to Gabe, Jamie, and the Silers Bald gang (not to mention the promoters and audiences) for the tremendous leap of faith that was that first tour.

The next year I wrote the rest of the songs: "So Long, Moses," "Labor of Love," and, finally, "Behold the Lamb of God." If you're paying attention, you'll notice that the first year we did a show called "Behold the Lamb of God" *without* a song called "Behold the Lamb of God." It was like taking off on an airplane and frantically assembling the landing gear at 20,000 feet. I didn't mention the fact that the bass player for Silers Bald was a young woman named Laura Story. Yes, *that* Laura Story.[3] Since my songwriting juices were depleted, I scribbled

---

3. Laura went on to do a few more tours with me, and on one of them she, Eric Peters, Ben Shive, and I decided to form a little songwriting club. We agreed to try and write a song a week, and to share them with each other. Laura was driving to my house from South Carolina, and as she wound through that gorgeous stretch of Interstate 40 between Asheville and Knoxville that carries you through the heart of the Smokies, she wrote the song "Indescribable." She pulled up to our house just in time for our songwriting powwow in the living room, and said, "Hey, guys. I wrote this on the way here. I don't

out the lyric for the chorus of "Behold the Lamb" and in about ten minutes she had written the melody that we still sing every year.

That second year was when we decided to put on a special show in Nashville. I invited Ron Block, Phil Keaggy, Fernando Ortega, and Jill Phillips to join us, we sold it out, and played more or less what the show is now, twenty years later. That was also the night I asked Ben Shive to join me on the road, and a few years later we were in the studio recording it with him and Andrew Osenga at the helm.

The barrage of names and dates and locations I just threw at you makes it all sound so fast. It wasn't. Between the time I started writing the songs and the day we released the album, I could have gotten another bachelor's degree. Jamie and I had another kid. We bought our first house. I released my first two label albums and toured constantly. Life happened. But each year we came back together in December to sing about the Incarnation.

Fighting through month after month of trying to pay the bills on the road, singing songs on my other albums about life and love and struggle, then coming back together each December to sing about Jesus and only about Jesus was like performing yearly maintenance on my soul. Every December I would think,

---

know if it's any good." And she sang the words, "From the highest of heights to the depth of the sea / all creation's revealing your majesty." Well, it was good. Chris Tomlin thought so, at least, along with a zillion churches across America. I'll always count it a privilege to have been one of the first to hear that wonderful song.

"Oh, right. *This* is the point of it all. Now I remember." It was like bringing flowers to my first love on our anniversary.

Actually, no. It was like my first love bringing flowers to me.

When the time finally came to record the album, we had done four tours. We had shaped the arrangements, figured out tempos, landed on harmonies, and tested it all on the road. But it wasn't until Andrew Osenga, Ben Shive, and I were in a basement studio late one night that the remnant of Extreme finally bubbled to the surface in its hair-metal glory. Up to that point we had been ending the show with "Joy to the World," and it worked, but I wanted to find a way to tie all the songs together somehow. We named the work track "Silent Majesty" as a joke (an obscure reference to *Christmas Vacation*), then came up with a chord progression and stacked lyrics from the key songs on top of one another until we found a cool way to build to the final, explosive reprise of, "Sing out with joy for the brave little boy who was God, but he made himself nothing."

At last, my nerdy high school dreams had come true. It was a proper concept album. But my college dreams came true, too, because it was also a proper Bible album, unabashedly about the Israelites and the Incarnation. And my musician dreams came true because it had dobros and mandolins and dulcimers thrown in with the strings and electric guitars. Come to think of it, it answered my longing for a community because so many friends came together to make the record, and then tour it, and those friendships deepened and deepened over the years. "God, will you let me sing about you?" I asked when I was nineteen. In some ways, his answer was *Behold the Lamb of*

God—which turned out to be so much more than I could have asked or imagined.

The whole thing has been such a gift. Not only did the Christmas tour carry my family through some really lean years, not only did it reset my heart's compass to the true north of the gospel, it also gave me the great gift of friendship. It wasn't so much generosity on my part that led to the community culture around this tour; it was necessity. There was simply no way I could pull off the concert alone. It had to be a community effort. And that led to the idea of the tour having the in-the-round component, which turned out to be one of the best things about it.

Each year we bring out a little slice of this sweet community of artists and musicians who genuinely love Jesus, and we tell *his* story. It hasn't always been fun. Touring is hard. Our kids have never known a December where their papa was home. We miss plays, church concerts, Christmas parties. I miss Jamie and the kids, and I know they miss me. I'm sure the rest of the band feels the same. But it's so very clear that this tour is a calling. How can I keep myself from singing?

During that chaotic rehearsal in 2000 I remember saying to Gabe, "Wouldn't it be cool to do this at the Ryman someday?" He agreed, and we stood there in a daze, imagining it for a moment before getting back to work.

Five years later, to our shock and delight, it happened. We stood on that stage among the ghosts of Johnny Cash and Rich Mullins, looking out at the same view Carolyn Arends had seen all those years ago. I walked around backstage and stood in the exact place where I met Rich in 1995, marveling at how good the Lord is.

Now, in our twentieth year of the tour, we play the Ryman as a matter of course. It's familiar territory. And I can tell you it's never, ever gotten old. Standing on that stage while the crowd sings the doxology at the end is a thunderously good feeling, not only because it sounds so nice but because it reminds me that God sometimes gives us exactly what we asked for, and then some.

Here's the point. If I had waited until the songs were finished, this thing might never have happened. If I had merely tinkered with these songs for all the years it took to finally record them, chances are I would have moved on to other things and never given it a try. It wouldn't have grown into what it was meant to be. You can think and plan and think some more, but none of that is half as important as *doing* something, however imperfect or incomplete it is. Intention trumps execution, remember? Sometimes you book the tour before the songs are written. Sometimes you stand at the altar and say "I do" without any clue how you and your wife are going to make it. Sometimes you move to Nashville with no money in the bank and no real prospects. Sometimes you start with nothing and hope it all works out. Not sometimes—*every* time. All you really have is your willingness to fail, coupled with the mountain of evidence that the Maker has never left nor forsaken you.

I used to stress out at the Ryman show. Will people like it as much as last year? Will it work again? Will everybody remember their parts? It was exhausting. Until one year I got sick and lost my voice the night before the concert. I looked around at the community gathered backstage—Jill, Andy, Gabe, Ben, Andrew, and all the others—and realized the show would go off without a hitch whether I was there or not. They're professionals. They're servants. They're more than capable, and they're more than willing to stand in the gap. I ended up being able to sing that night, but that year and every year since my enjoyment of the show was amplified by the simple truth that it's not my show at all. I'm pleasantly expendable, delightfully unnecessary.

We're not invited into this because God needs us, but because he *wants* us.

In the words of Laura Story, all creation's revealing his majesty. We're invited to join with all nature in manifold witness to his great faithfulness—and since creation is going to declare it either way, we might as well jump in with our half-finished songs and join the chorus.

5

A MATTER OF LIFE OR DEATH

When I was a freshman in high school I got a Yamaha scooter for my birthday. Actually I bought it for a few hundred bucks earned from my job at the grocery store. The birthday present was my dad's acquiescence to a year's worth of begging and badgering for permission to buy the nerdy little thing.

It was a funny looking machine, not much more substantial than a bicycle, but it topped out at a mind-blowing 35 mph, which to my delight was fast enough to get hurt. I drove it to school and was immediately the object of much ridicule—internal ridicule, that is, because I have no memory of anyone ever actually ridiculing me. But memories of self-consciousness abound and I'm sure I projected all sorts of judgmental stares and mutterings from my friends, many of whom drove 4x4 trucks and had ATVs at their disposal. But that little scooter might as well have been a magic portal for all the escape it provided.

After I puttered home from school and dropped off my book bag I would ride that thing like a cowboy on his trusty steed all over the back roads of Lake Butler. And in a little town like that, back roads were easy to find. Because I was (and still am) a very private person, I usually struck out for the least populated parts of town, far away from the stares of the townsfolk. Most often, I drove north to the lake, turned right, and headed a few miles into the country along the east side of the lake, where at the Arnold farm I took a left onto a sandy road that led into the pines of the Wildlife Management Area. Those roads crisscrossed and wound and rambled for miles, and eventually connected to the highway on the opposite side of the lake, several miles away. It was easy to get lost, but if you drove for long enough you'd eventually spot the swampy lake shore or a familiar crossroads and make your way either back to where you started or at least to a highway that would lead you safely home.

One afternoon I brought a blue folder that held several pages of blank notebook paper. I had a Bic pen in my back pocket. It was cold—cold for Florida, anyway—and by the time I found my way back to the hard road near the Arnold farm the sun was setting. On the north side of the road there's a wide field bordered by a dark wall of pine trees, and at this time of year there was soybean growing in bright green rows. Over that field and beyond the veil of pines I caught sight of a blazing sky and stopped the scooter in the middle of the road, tingling with some awareness of holiness, of rare and unlooked-for beauty. I steered the scooter off the road and through the gate, then drove carefully between the planted rows till I found a suitable spot, aware of how conspicuous the scooter's head-light must have been from the distant farmhouse. I turned the key and silenced the pleasant purr of the engine, then removed my helmet and flipped down the kickstand, easing it into the dark soil. I sat down between two rows and pulled the pen out of the back pocket of my Levi's as I opened the blue folder. I looked up at the sunset, which was already changing colors. I was wonderfully alone, and yet the air was charged with a strange light that suggested anything but aloneness. I tried to write down what I saw, and what I felt, and what the holy presence that was bringing about the evolution of color might have been telling me. Every time I looked up from the words on the paper, the sky looked different, and I tried to get it all down—all the changes, all the beauty, all the life suggested by the fading day and the brightening of the clouds. The colors were azure and lavender, not just blue and purple. The clouds were feathery and flaming, not just soft and yellow. In a way that I had never experienced before, the loveliness of the light demanded new adjectives. In a way that I had never experienced before, I felt God's presence as a pleasant fire that called for obedience and energy and expression.

You have to understand: I was at the time enraptured with comic books and fantasy novels. I had never read Annie Dillard or Frederick Buechner or (other than Narnia) C. S. Lewis. I had no context for the kind of writing that attempted to capture in words either the burning beauty of a Florida sunset or the God who had lit the fire. But I filled a page with words, with weak and overwrought sentences; like a juggler who kept fumbling I scratched out words and wrote what I thought were better ones, aiming at something excellent even as I was aware of how pathetically short I fell. It didn't matter that I would prob- ably never show anyone what I had written, though I admit I harbored a wild hope that this page of words was important somehow, even if it would only ever be important to me. I saw something beautiful, felt something profound, and was compelled to express it on paper. I spoke aloud to the pres- ence that designed this picture frame, the God of the Bible who first imagined pigment itself. I spoke sheepishly at first, then with increasing boldness as I became convinced that no human was eavesdropping. The loneliness of the dark field was a prerequisite for the company I felt. These words were between you, Master, and me. (I am aware even now on this wintry afternoon in Nashville of that same presence reading over my shoulder, and am obliged to acknowledge his patient and peaceful attention.)

When the sunset had played itself out and the first stars of evening shone, I closed the folder, slipped the pen back into my pocket, and straddled the scooter. I listened to the silence framed by cricket song, then with regret that the moment was over, kick-started the Yamaha. I bounced out of the field and onto the smooth tarmac, then sped home only realizing by my sniffles that tears had come to my eyes.

A few days later, my parents found the notebook and read my words. I was intensely embarrassed, and though I don't remember telling them so, it felt as though someone had seen me naked. They didn't make fun. They probably encouraged my writing. But I still felt violated. The words weren't for them— they were intended to be for myself and my God, and so I vowed to be even more guarded with my deepest thoughts. This was something precious and private, and the next time I wrote something like this I couldn't shake the feeling that someone, sometime, would read the words and pass some sort of judgment on them, or on me.

And yet, here I am, telling you about it.

I've spent the last twenty years arranging words, not just with the awareness that someone might read them over my shoulder, but with the intention of having them read. Now, when I write my prayers, when I spot an intense beauty burning at the roadside and am moved to write about it, I obey the compulsion but promptly delete the file. I could fill a book with those deleted files.

If I write something to be sung or read, it's with a different mind-set altogether, a constantly edited voice, with the eyes of my little town watching the strange boy with the strange scooter and wondering what strange thing he's up to. I'm more likely to follow the rules—their rules—and I seldom abandon myself to the work at hand with that same childlike effusion of praise.

Has this made me a better writer, or a worse one?

Sometimes I long to escape to the woods again. To be who I was that night in the field, fumbling the ball and still fighting to express back to God the wonder of human praise, to limn some reflection of the gift of light he gave, to speak without fear of ridicule. To sit in the dusk and feel that same lonesome freedom of intimacy with the One who knows me and is— astonishingly—well pleased. To weep without knowing it, to obey the whispered will of the Spirit: *Look out over the field to your right. Leave the well-traveled road. Quiet the engine. Sit in the fertile dirt and listen. Watch how time changes the light, how steadily the firmament burns. Know that I am with you always, and let that knowledge find life in the best words you can find.*

——————

A few years ago I had lunch with a friend in Chattanooga. His name is Chris Slaten, and he's an excellent songwriter performing under the name Son of Laughter. I'm envious of his beard. I asked him how his songwriting was going, and since he's a schoolteacher I wondered where and when he wrote. Did he have an office? He smiled between bites of tortilla chips and tapped his temple. "I do it up here," he said.

This may come as a surprise to you, that a song could be written in that miraculous space between a human's ears. It surprises me, even though I've done it before. Chris said that the other day he had a doctor's appointment and he sat in the waiting room with a copy of Hemingway's *For Whom the Bell Tolls*. He opened the book for a moment, then shut it and decided instead to work on a song. He stared at a fake plant in the corner for twenty minutes and bent his will to the task. He said he was sure that he looked strange, staring all that time without really moving. But he made progress. He got home, grabbed his guitar, and tested out what he had "written," then helped his wife with dinner until the next time he had twenty minutes to think—which was, he said, the next morning's commute to the school.

If you wait until the conditions are perfect, you'll never write a thing.

It's always a matter of the will. The songs won't create themselves, and neither will the books, the recipes, the blue-prints, or the gardens. One of my favorite poems by one of my favorite poets, Richard Wilbur, is called "The Writer." Look it up. Seriously. Right now, go find a computer, google it, and read it twice. Then head over to a bookstore and buy his collected poems. Keep the book on your nightstand and read one of them each night before you sleep. Writing is always a matter of life or death, he says, and finding the right arrangements of words is like being a bird trapped in a house, trying to find its way through the open window.

When I was in college, as I said, I wrote most of my songs during class. I often sat next to my friend CJ, who was not only my college roommate, but was the guy who taught me to play the guitar ten years earlier at church camp. The first song I ever learned on the guitar was "Patience," by Guns 'n Roses, which starts in the key of C with a whistle solo, and I must say that there are much worse first songs a guy could have learned. CJ, who was hard at work learning to write songs even in high school, also happens to be the guy who introduced me to the music of Rich Mullins. I have happy memories of the music we made at CJ's house during his senior year of high school. We'd pull out the guitars and Belinda, his mom, would belt out "Lovin', Touchin', Squeezin'" by Journey. Man, did she have some pipes. The whole family did. Those "na-na-na's" at the end of the song provided me one of my first opportunities to sing harmony. I was the skinny kid in the background, trying to keep up, trying to learn to sing in tune.

When I look back at those days I'm overwhelmed by their kindness. The Fluhartys encouraged me to sing, to play, to write, even though I was sloppy and flat and overeager. When CJ graduated high school and went to Bible College, I followed suit, partly because I had nothing better to do.

So there we sat next to each other in Old Testament survey classes, covertly passing lyrics back and forth. I watched the way he wrote his songs, the way he ordered the words on the page, arranging the stanzas so he could keep track of the meter of each line, the way he anguished over the syncopation of the syllables. I had still not managed to finish a song of my own—nothing worth sharing, anyway—but I felt a burning desire to contribute to our little college band's body of work.

I was a freshman, and fresh out of a pretty intense relationship with a girl. Then along came Jamie. She was beautiful and funny and full of life. She was a junior, and it was impossible to ignore her. We fell in love in a matter of weeks, and I knew without a doubt that if we kept dating we'd be married before you could sing the chorus of "Patience."

That was what scared me.

I had just started college, I had dreams of playing music with a band, and was utterly unprepared to marry anybody, even if she was beautiful and wonderful and encouraging beyond measure. There were days when I wished I could retreat to a simpler place where there were no big decisions to be made. These are the lyrics I worked on for those early weeks of college.

I take a walk down a dusty road and I
Sink my feet in memories of colder days gone by
I don't want to go, but it's all downhill
And it seems so easy, I think I will
Go down

Could you tell that I'd been crying
When you talked to me today?
I'd been running from the words inside
I never meant to say

So come on with me and I'll walk you around
Through the backstreets of this old ghost town
Come along and you will see
There's a place where we can be
Far away from you and me
Way down

I'll spare you the rest. To be honest, reading it now I don't really know what it means. Something about memories, something melodramatic about wanting to escape all the questions so we could just hang out like the lovebirds we were. Apparently there was some kind of tearful discussion about our future, but I don't remember it now.

I don't mean to diminish what must have felt at the time like a big deal, but the obscurity of the lyric makes it difficult for me to take it seriously. There are two more verses equally vague and earnest, but at the time I couldn't find the chorus. One afternoon in apartment 418 my nineteen-year-old self mustered the courage to play my unfinished song for CJ and ask him what he thought. Where should the chorus go? What should it be about? Was this all terrible?

No, he said, it wasn't a bad start. He liked it in all its Toad the Wet Sprocket-ripoff glory. He looked over the lyrics, pointed at the part about the ghost town that ended with "way down" and said, "That's your chorus. It already has one." Then he took a bite out of his apple and walked over to the courtyard picnic table with his guitar to work on a song of his own.

Sometimes you've done all the planting you need to do, and it's time to start weeding the garden.

Steven Pressfield's book *The War of Art* describes what he calls "Resistance," a mysterious force in the world that seems to challenge every creative act. Pressfield isn't a Christian, as far as I know, but when he talks about the way we have to fight an opposing force in order to bring something beautiful into the world, I resonate. I believe there's a Resistance, and it's made up of what Paul called the rulers, the authorities, the cosmic powers over this present darkness, the spiritual forces of evil in the heavenly places (Eph. 6:12). If you're called to speak light into the darkness, then believe this: the darkness wants to shut you up. Even now I can feel the strength of Resistance. Every sentence feels like a wobbly step. Everything I think feels obvious, pointless, silly. I take comfort in what I've written before, but it's a fool's comfort; just because God graced me with some insight in the past doesn't mean I'm special or insightful. I only got there in the first place because of a desperate need of grace. So I pray, right now, as I'm writing this, for the grace to say something helpful to the reader, so that he or she might be encouraged in their own struggle to push forward into another day. That's what I want, after all. This is not an exercise in self-promotion or self-indulgence. This is for *you*. Whoever you are. Even if *you* means the future me. I cannot allow these thoughts to fester in isolation. They must be shared, aimed outward, scattered wild in the wind for some soul to discover.

As I've said, art shouldn't be about self-expression or self-indulgence. Art shouldn't be about self. The paradox is that art is necessarily created by a Self, and will necessarily draw some measure of attention or consideration to the artist. But the aim ought to be for the thing to draw attention, ultimately, to something other than the Self. For a Christian, that means accepting this paradox in the knowledge, or at least in the hope, that my expression, even if it is of the most intimate chambers of my heart, can lead the audience beyond me and to the Ultimate Self, the Word that made the world. In that grand chamber alone will art find its best end, as an avenue to lead the audience Home.

Lead me home, Jesus. Let me die to my need to be someone important. Let me die to my need to leave a mark.

Over the gateway of Self is a sign that says, "Abandon hope, all ye who enter." It is a hellish, helpless place. Die to self. Live to God. Let your words and music be more beautiful by their death in the soil of worship, that the husk of your own imperfection might fall away and germinate into some bright, eternal song only God could have written.

We must resist Resistance.

Tonight I was talking to my daughter about self-consciousness. She was laughing about how hard it is to pay attention to what someone's saying once you realize that you're paying attention to what someone's saying. I knew exactly what she was talking about.

When my mind is fatigued at the end of a concert or at church or whatever and I'm talking to someone, the merest thought of my weariness, or what's going on at home or how hungry I am or how nice it'll be to be alone in the hotel lobby reading a book, creates an almost painful charade of attention. They're talking; I do, in fact, usually care about what they're saying. But the space between my eyebrows starts to ache because I'm forcing myself to stare at their eyes. Stare at their eyes. Keep staring at their eyes. Show them how kind and interested I am. Of course, now I'm not really listening to what they're telling me. I have fallen by the wayside and am lost in the tangled brush of Self.

This is all obvious.

Here's the thing I wanted to tell you. Once I was doing a photo shoot—and before you roll your eyes and call me pretentious, you should know that I truly hate photo shoots, or I used to before the thing happened that I'm about to tell you. I only bring it up because it's crucial to the point. So there I was, wearing clothes some fashion person bought for me, sucking in my gut because the jeans didn't fit, worrying about my hopelessly frizzy, poofy, cowlicky hair, knowing without a doubt that the record label was wasting good money trying to make me look cool so they could sell more records. (True confession: sometimes they make you wear makeup.) Sometimes there are five people looking at you objectively, cocking their heads sideways and considering the waistline pudge you wish you had jogged off six months ago. My lowest-selling album is also the only one with my face on the cover, so I have to assume some correlation.

My manager's then-assistant Andrea happened to be there and I grumbled to her about being self-conscious. She used to do drama and she told me about an exercise she did with her troupe.

"Just think about the other person," she said. "It's easy. Two people stand on the stage and describe everything the *other* person is doing. Like this. 'You're standing there and your left hand is in your pants pocket and you're pacing. Now you're looking around. You're scratching the back of your head.' And as soon as you start talking about the other person, you stop looking awkward and self-conscious. You look like *you*. It's all about the other person."

It works. That was the last photo shoot I hated. Don't get me wrong—I'd still rather be doing almost anything else. But now when I stand there in the fancy clothes ("shoot loot," they call it) I try hard to think about the photographer, about my wife, about the kind folks who are working to get my songs heard by more people, and I stop caring quite so much about whether I'm standing awesomely. This is me, for better or for worse.

Once again, Jesus was right all along. We are most ourselves when we're thinking least about ourselves. It reminds me of Paul's rant in Romans 7, when he talks about how he wants to do one thing but then does another, and you can just hear his frustration with himself. That passage has brought me such comfort merely through commiseration. But it's really a passage about self-consciousness. At the end he asks, "Who will save me from this body of death?" (v. 24). And his answer is almost a sigh of relief: "Thanks be to God through Jesus Christ our Lord!" (v. 25). Self, self, self—then Christ, Christ, Christ. Paul, who for a paragraph seems almost pathetic in his self-frustration, turns his eyes to Christ and then reminds himself and the rest of us that there is no condemnation for those who are in Christ Jesus. Tear your attention away from your shame, your self-loathing, your self-consciousness, your *self*. Now, rejoice. Become who you were meant to be, who you already are in Christ. Then get busy writing. Park the scooter in the field and write with abandon. Fight back. It's a matter of life and death.

I still don't like photo shoots, though.

6

LONGING TO BELONG

I was born homesick. Maybe we all were. In 2006 I was in our subdivision house on Harbor Lights Drive, holed up in the spare bedroom-turned-office while the kids bumped around in the living room and Jamie cooked dinner. When I read the last few paragraphs of Wendell Berry's towering novel *Jayber Crow* I felt such an overwhelming collision of sadness and joy that I literally slid out of my chair and curled up on the floor, weeping in a patch of sunlight. Other than the end of *The Lord of the Rings* and *The Chronicles of Narnia* I'd never been so leveled by a book.

But why? I wondered. What was it about this particular book that resonated with me so? If I ask myself the same question about Narnia and Middle-earth, the answer becomes clearer: I wanted to find my way through the wardrobe; I wanted to sail with Frodo to the Grey Havens. I longed to *belong*. *Jayber Crow* is about a lot of things, but one of its major themes is community, or in Wendell Berry parlance, *membership*—by which he means belonging to both a people *and* a place. Looking back, I realize I've always been on the hunt for belonging. We left small town Illinois when I was seven and, though I really tried to make it work, small-town Florida never felt like home. I lived a sort of half-life there through middle and high school, and got out of Dodge as soon as I could. Jamie and I ended up in Nashville, where we've stayed long enough that at least all our kids can say they belong to a place. They've always lived within a few miles of where they were born. It's a start.

During our first ten years here, our family lived in four different houses. We liked the adventure of a new place. But after *Jayber Crow* I was done with transience. I was stirred by a longing to care for the land under my feet, to work in partnership with the earth instead of in opposition to it, to learn the names of the birds and the flora and fauna as well as the names of my neighbors, and to shepherd some corner of this planet for the sake of the Kingdom. As far as it was in my limited power to do so, I wanted to mend the world—even if it was just a few acres of it.

As nice as it was to live in a little Nashville subdivision, pushing a stroller through the neighborhood in the evening and being close enough to Percy Priest Lake to take our little Sunfish sailboat out at a moment's notice, Jamie and I both knew it wasn't the house we wanted to die in. Our neighborhood, like so many subdivisions, practically embodied the word *transitory*. Neighbors came and went. New streets were always being carved out of the tree line. Every other day, it seemed, a "For Sale" sign showed up in someone's yard. It wasn't the kind of place we could imagine our grandchildren getting excited to visit.

By then, several of our friends had moved to East Nashville, where at the time you could still buy a pretty bungalow and renovate it on the cheap. There were cool restaurants and historic neighborhoods (a little known fact: the outlaw Jesse James lived there for a while when he was on the lam). Now East Nashville is the hipster center of town and the bungalows are priced like mansions, so we missed that boat. Then one day we visited my old roommate Mark (the same Mark who picked me up from the bus station and helped me record my indy EP all those years ago) because he had just moved with his wife and kids to a farmhouse in South Nashville. Only minutes from the city, a winding road took us past cattle ponds and ramshackle barns, over bridges that spanned Mill Creek, and finally up a gravel drive to their hundred-year-old farmhouse. As soon as we arrived, I broke the tenth commandment. Sort of. I didn't exactly covet my neighbor's house, but I coveted the land. I coveted the peace and quiet, the story of the farm, the stands of hackberry and white oak and cedar. I immediately wanted to move there. By this time I had found in Nashville a people to belong to—could this be the place?

I sat on their front porch, eyeing a little house across the pasture. "Do you think any of your neighbors will ever sell?" He told me it was doubtful since the other houses on the hill were occupied by members of the family that had grown up there. But, come to think of it, the old cabin at the top of the hill was for sale. Jamie and I drove up and checked it out, but it was on twelve acres and well out of our price range. As we disappointedly crunched back down the gravel drive I had a vision. It burned itself into my imagination so brightly that I can still see it now, clear as day. I saw Skye as a little pigtailed girl in overalls tearing through the meadow in the spring, the air full of sunlit pollen. Even as I pictured it I grieved because it didn't seem possible that we'd ever live there. So we kept looking. I continued to wrestle with my discontent: Was it worldliness or was it the Holy Spirit pulling me toward something? I just couldn't tell.

Then about a year later, Mark called and said his neighbors had in fact decided to sell, at a price we just might be able to afford. Jamie and I met with the owners, then we drove out there every day for weeks, dreaming, wondering, praying. I drove friends out to show them the property, asking their opinions, seeking wisdom. One day Jason Gray and I sat on the front porch of what would one day be our home and he prayed that God would give us the wisdom to know if we should try to buy it.

The catch was, the house was 25 percent smaller than our current one. And it wasn't exactly pretty. The kitchen was literally the size of a walk-in closet and the décor wasn't, shall we say, "aligned with Jamie's taste." But the building itself wasn't what interested me. All I could see when I looked out the front window was that daydream of Skye's pigtails bouncing through the meadow. (The boys probably weren't in the daydream because they were busy building forts in the daydream woods.)

In the end, we went for it. Without knowing America was on the verge of the Great Recession, we sold our subdivision home for a tiny profit and bought a house in one of the last rural pockets of Davidson County. The day we moved in, Jamie cried. They weren't happy tears, mind you. Our kids were growing by the minute, I was touring more or less constantly, and we had just done a very un-American thing: we had down-sized. We had also down-*styled*. The old vinyl flooring was, well, old. One corner of the outdated carpet had been chewed up by the former owners' cat. The kitchen, as I said, was miniscule. None of this would have been hard for her except that we had gotten used to the relative niceness of the subdivision house. "But look at the *land*," I would say, encouragingly, with a grand sweep of my hand. Bless her heart, she took a deep breath and dug in. I love that woman.

"Can we please replace the carpet sooner rather than later?" she asked on the day we closed.

"Of course," I said without really looking at how bad the carpet was. "We'll get to it." My mind was on cutting trails and building tree houses. I went out for a weekend of shows and came home to a shock. There was a pile of old carpet in the front yard. Jamie had singlehandedly torn it up and hauled it out with an iron will.

"Now. About that carpet," she said with a smile. "Here are some choices for hardwood flooring." Like I said, I love that woman. Without delay, she began making our house beautiful. And I started reclaiming the land. When we moved in I was finishing my first reading of Richard Adams's master-piece *Watership Down*, about a community of rabbits on a great journey to find a new warren. Not only was our new place built on the side of a very English-looking down, there were always rabbits in the front pasture.

We named our place The Warren—not only because our journey mirrored Hazel and Fiver's, and not only because of the rabbits that abounded, but because the new house was so small that there were times—especially when the kids had friends over and it was too rainy to play outside and we were stepping on Legos and bumping into each other in the tiny kitchen—when we felt like we were living in a little under-ground rabbit hole.

Don't get me wrong. I know many people don't have homes at all, so I shouldn't be complaining about the size or weird layout of the house. I'm just saying that downsizing ain't easy, especially with three small children. *Especially*-especially when one of the two parents has a job that requires weeks of travel. (Sorry, Jamie.) But when the kids came in with skinned knees from climbing trees, or when the sun threw golden light at the hill in the late afternoon and we all went out to watch the clouds catch fire, or when we woke in the misty morning and walked the trails in Warren Wood and saw the kids' tree forts quietly awaiting their return, or when we sat on the porch on warm nights and listened to the barred owls calling to each other from the dark branches, we knew we had chosen wisely. God had provided a place we could love, a place our grandchildren could love as much as our children did. About five years in, we were able to build an addition that made the inside as lovely as the outside—and once again it was because Jamie, too, had a picture in her mind, and did the hard, creative work of incarnating it.

I tell you all this because place *matters*.

Of course, not everyone can move to the country, nor should they. But wherever you are, you might as well go ahead and pull up the carpet. Make it beautiful, even if you can't afford it. Let your imagination run wild. Give your house a name. Watch how it changes the way you treat it. *Let thy Kingdom come, thy will be done, in our house as it is in heaven.* I started keeping bees. Those bees pollinate the flowers we put in the ground. I planted apple, plum, pear, and peach trees, blueberries, raspberries, and blackberries that feed the people who tend these acres.

Jamie hung pictures on the walls. She keeps candles lit in whatever room we're hanging out in, year-round. If we ever move (and I hope we don't) we will have left our mark on this home and on this property—in the same way our children, who are too old to play in the woods anymore, have left behind clubhouses and stone paths and *Wizard of Oz* signs nailed to the trees that say, "HAUNTED FOREST" and "I'D TURN BACK IF I WERE YOU." When I walk the trails now I can hear the memory of their laughter echoing in the trees. We have become members of this place, members of this community, of this Kingdom—praying his will to be done in these woods as it is in heaven.

I met Julie Witmer at Hutchmoot[4] several years ago. She's from Pennsylvania. She has an English gardener's certificate, and called one day to ask if she could give our family a gift.

She and her family came down to stay with us one weekend, and she and her husband James spent hours walking the property, taking measurements, scribbling notes in a little journal. About three months later we received a tubular package in the mail. We opened it and were awestruck as we spread out on our kitchen table a hand-drawn schematic of The Warren. Julie called it a thirty-year garden plan. All around the drawing of our house were colorful splotches representing alchemilla, coneflowers, clematis, yarrow, lavender, foxgloves, and all manner of trees and shrubs, all divided by walkways and places for firepits and benches. On the right of the drawing was a list of the plants and how many of each we would need. One of the difficulties of landscaping a few acres is that it's too much space to know what to do with. On the other hand, while designing a small front garden isn't easy, at

4. Hutchmoot is the ridiculously wonderful name for the annual Rabbit Room conference. More on that later.

least you know the boundaries. We had a big pasture that took me four hours to mow. So Julie hemmed things in by telling us where to build fences and stone walls immediately around the house, with paths that led to the broader sections. She gave us a picture frame so we would know where to paint.

What a gift.

I framed the drawing and hung it on the wall by the front door, in a place where I'd see it every time I left the house. I spent hours staring at it, looking up from the drawing to the yard, then back at the drawing again, dreaming of the day when I could walk around in what she had imagined. After a year or so of putting it off, I decided it was time to start with the front garden. Julie had drawn a stone wall enclosing a rectangular space right out front. The space was divided into quadrants by a T-shaped pea gravel walkway with a stone feature at the intersection. But how do you build a wall? I had seen enough of them in England (and Nashville) to know that a stone wall is a beautiful thing (whatever Robert Frost might have thought), and I wanted one. But I didn't have a clue how to go about it. So I dug around on the Internet and learned that if you hire a professional a dry stack stone wall costs about $100 per foot. This wall was at least 100 feet long, and while I'm no math genius I knew that would be about $10,000. No way on earth I could afford that. The garden plan, however, only worked if it was enclosed. It had to be done, and if this plan was going to take thirty years I needed to get started, *stat*. I could have cheated and just built a fence, true, but my inner perfectionist wasn't having it.

One day I passed a pile of throwaway rocks on the side of the road, so I pulled over and loaded them into my pickup. The next day I saw another pile, then another, and loaded them both. You wouldn't believe how much unwanted stone is just lying around in Tennessee. The next time I walked around our woods I noticed a ton (literally) of rocks scattered about the property, so I loaded them into a wheelbarrow and heaved them up to the front yard. The kids had a list of daily chores anyway, so I added the assignment of walking the woods each morning and bringing two rocks each day to the pile. Then, satisfied that I had enough to get started, I watched hours of YouTube videos about dry stack walls.

During a warm snap in January I walked outside with a shovel and dug the first footer for the foundation. I figured we had enough rocks piled up to make some real progress, but after fussing with it for a few chilly hours I had gone through all our rocks and had completed about six feet of two-foot-high wall. Just 94 feet to go. I thought about Roy Scheider in *Jaws* and said to myself, "We're gonna need more rocks." My obsessive nature kicked in, and I spent weeks scouring the Nashville area for more stones. I pilfered construction sites, walked the woods around our house for hours, searched the shoulders of highways—and discovered treasure troves of discarded stones, which I surreptitiously hauled away in my old truck. Years later, I still can't help but notice orphaned stones beside the road, and my kids still make fun of me.

Slowly but surely, the wall took shape. My arms did, too, to Jamie's delight. At some point I got it into my head that the wall needed an archway—as in, a *bona fide* Roman Arch, suspended by nothing but a keystone and this thing called gravity. Once again, YouTube provided all I really needed to know. I built up the sides of an opening, then measured and built a wooden frame with a round top. By now my older brother decided he needed to come over and inform me in classic older-brother fashion that it would never work—which, of course, was all the motivation I needed to carry through. I stacked the stones on top of the frame, set the keystone, and used a hammer to tighten it all with little shims of flinder. When all was ready, with the whole family watching, I nervously removed the legs from the frame. The round wooden support fell away, and—lo, and behold!—the thing held. My brother grunted something congratulatory and went home as I high-fived Jamie and the kids.

It took another few weeks to complete the other arm of the wall, and before long the footpaths were dug, some plants were in the ground, and we had an actual enclosed cottage garden, complete with a stone archway, right here at The Warren.

It's no exaggeration to say that it was a spiritual experience. I couldn't stop thinking about songwriting, about creativity, and especially about the New Creation. Julie dreamed up a better world for us; we had been commissioned, so to speak, to look at the world we occupied in a new way, and to incarnate that vision; whenever I looked out my window I saw the same old field, but one quick glance at the framed plan on the wall reminded me where we were going and whispered encouragement to get busy; I had been invited into a better story, and the only way to tell it was to get my hands dirty (and to appropriate some rocks); and even though Julie designed the thing without a stone arch, she encouraged me to bring my own imagination to bear on the project, to make the changes I saw fit, and to let the garden become what it wanted to become.

I finished the wall that spring around Easter, and one morning I woke at dawn, just as the sun broke over the hill and shot a ray of new light across the property. Because the earth had been slowly tilting its way toward summer, that light landed in a new place, illuminating the stone arch. I peeked through the blinds and gasped, because the arch, suspended by gravity (a delightfully poetic thought) looked like the mouth of the empty tomb. Those rocks, repurposed and reborn, were crying out praise.

Lenten Sonnet
March 8, 2017

This morning I woke and opened the shade,
Saw frost in the shadows, dew in the light,
Steam hovering up through each gleaming blade
Of grass. The stone arch caught the sun. The sight
Of it all, first thing in the morning, wakes
A contentment with the world. I feel young
Knowing the slow turn of the planet rakes
A bright edge of infant light, a tune sung
As long as the world has spun: new again,
New again, the mercies of God are new
Each morning, and morning moves with the spin
Of the old earth and greets each eye on cue—
Mercy, speeding west from here to the plain
To the peaks, to the sea, then back again.

I love this place. I love it because I have loved it with my labor, with sweat and blood and a persistent longing to belong to it. My name is on the deed, which means I own it, inasmuch as a human can own a part of the earth. It belongs to me more than any place I've ever known—but in a deeper, truer way, I belong to it. In the honey from my bees and the bounty from the berry bushes I have literally tasted the fruit of my co-laboring with this corner of creation, and it is profoundly sweet. It speaks to me of its Maker. And my Maker speaks to me through it. I love to watch people taste my honey. They always close their eyes and breathe deep, and they always proclaim it better by far than whatever they buy at the grocery store. I'm not sure it tastes all that different, but their enjoyment is heightened by the knowledge that it came from the flowers underfoot and the long labor of the bees' sweet alchemy. I think it reminds them of Eden. The world that is whispers of the world to come, just as Julie's thirty-year plan invites me into the long struggle of begetting something new and beautiful made out of Tennessee stones as old as Everest. The Kingdom is coming, but the Kingdom is here. That's why we're homesick, and it's also why we might as well get busy planting.

Rip out the carpet and let it be.

7

THE INTEGRATED IMAGINATION

My grandmother asked what kind of books I liked to read. "Fantasy novels," I said. I probably had a *Dragonlance* book hidden in my backpack, next to the Walkman with the Tesla tape, the *TransWorld Skateboarding* mag, and the Trapper Keeper with a Camaro on the front.

"Isn't that sort of thing for girls?" she asked. She tilted her head back to better see me through her glasses.

"What do you mean? There's nothing girly about them."

"Hmm." She went back to her game of solitaire while I tried to tone down my defensiveness.

"Granny, I'm serious. Lots of my friends read them, and I don't know a single girl who does."

"Well, I guess times have changed," she said with a sad little shake of her head.

We went back and forth for a few minutes before I realized that when I said "fantasy" she thought I meant romance, the steamy kind—you know, the paperbacks with the scarlet covers and flowing scripts, always with a ravished woman wrapped in the arms of a blond dude with breeches and riding boots and no shirt, muscles so big he could snap the ravished woman in half, and from the way she's looking at him it seems she wouldn't mind so much if he did. His name is probably Dirk. No wonder my grandmother looked worried.

"No, Granny," I said with relief. "Fantasy novels. Swords and dragons and stuff. The less romance the better." That wasn't strictly true, because in *Dragons of Autumn Twilight*, Tanis

Half-Elven and elf princess Lauralanthalasa (I'm not kidding) had a thing going, but they had to keep it quiet because her people mistrusted his half-humanness and it created all kinds of romantic tension, plus the War of the Lance interfered and all. But mostly there were dragons. And dwarves. And magic weapons and dungeons and taverns teeming with thieves and adventurers.

I remember Christmas morning 1987 when I tore the wrapping paper off of several *Dragonlance* books—books that I swore to my dad weren't the same as Dungeons & Dragons games, though it turned out they were. Almost exactly the same, in fact, but in book form. Even more startling, I didn't turn into a devil-worshipping delinquent, nor did the books spontaneously combust on the holy ground of the church parsonage. To the contrary, I'm in my forties now and I still remember the warm tingle in my fingers when I first held those pulp paperbacks. I can still smell them. If I close my eyes I can see the cover painting by a guy named Larry Elmore. It featured the aforementioned Tanis Half-Elven, Goldmoon the barbarian princess, and Sturm the warrior standing in an autumnal vale with a red dragon coiled behind them. The whole gang was looking at the camera, so to speak, as if waiting for me to step into the book and join them. Now it all seems so cliché, but at the time I didn't know and didn't care.

I filled notebooks with drawings of those dragons, talismans, old stone doorways, and walking lizards called Draconians. I thought about those stories in class, and read them after I failed tests, and talked about them with my brother and our nerdy friends while we built skateboard ramps in the garage. The books lifted me straight out of the mossy pines of North Florida and plopped me down in a magical world, just as surely as Lucy stepped through the wardrobe and found herself in Narnia. My young mind crackled with longing, though I wouldn't have known to call it that. I merely said to myself, "Man, that's so cool," in an awestruck whisper.

Not long after that, at my older brother's behest, I read David Eddings's *The Belgariad*, a five-book epic fantasy about a kid named Garion who eventually learns to speak a secret spy language with tiny movements of his fingers. If that weren't cool enough, he also saves the world by recovering an orb. I wonder how many times an imaginary world has been saved by the recovery of an orb? I loved these books almost as much as I loved the *Dragonlance Chronicles*. Around the same time I read Stephen King's *It* and *The Talisman* (which he wrote with Peter Straub), both of which ought to be considered fantasy novels, and neither of which are as good as I remember.

My brother also got me hooked on David Gerrold's *The War Against the Chttor* series, which launched me over to the somewhat parallel genre of science fiction. Gerrold's books explore everything from war tactics to ethics to religion to sexuality—but to my relief, there were also plenty of guns, zombies, and wormy critters that wanted to eat the world. Even so, there were moments of bliss when I closed my door at night, switched on the reading light, cracked open the paperback of *A Rage for Revenge*, and could almost hear the hiss of the pressurization system kicking on as I stepped onto the space transport. Gone were the humid bedsheets and the oscillating fan and the mossy trees of Florida, gone was my nascent fear that I would be miserable for the rest of my life, gone were my failures; I was saving the world, baby, and I might not make it back alive.

Then I'd wake on the ugly green couch in my room to the sound of my dad stomping through the house singing "Rise and shine, give God the glory-glory" in full preacher voice. It was time to embark on another day of school, another day of facing what felt like an enormous waste of time—except for those few minutes between failures when I could duck through the trapdoor of my book and emerge into a world of real beauty and real danger, which meant real heroism and the possibility of real purpose. I was hungry for it. Maybe even starving.

Every time we drove the thirty minutes to Gainesville, the nearest town with a mall, I headed straight for Waldenbooks. When I got to Waldenbooks I headed straight for the fantasy/sci-fi section, which at the time boasted only a few shelves. Always with a tantalizing fraction of that same tingle I felt on Christmas morning in 1987, I ran my fingers over the spines of all those paperbacks: Anne McCaffrey's *The Dragonriders of Pern*, Ursula K. LeGuin's *Earthsea Chronicles*, Lloyd Alexander's *Prydain Chronicles*, an ever increasing number of *Dragonlance* books (now there are about two hundred), the D&D spinoff *Forgotten Realms* (which I never cared for, though the covers were killer), Stephen R. Lawhead's *The Pendragon Cycle*, Robert Jordan's *The Eye of the World*, Terry Brooks's *The Sword of Shannara*, and of course, towering above them all, J. R. R. Tolkien's *The Lord of the Rings*—a book I hadn't read, which caused my brother no end of consternation. I had seen the animated films seven hundred times, so I didn't think I needed to read it yet. (Don't be angry.

Tolkien, for me, came later.) But hobbits aside, I stood in the aisle at Waldenbooks and *yearned*, I tell you. I was drawn to those book covers like a deer to a salt lick, and like a salt lick they only made me thirstier. I couldn't get enough.

In those days, I was restless without a book in my hands, without the hope of some new story around every turn to enliven my deadening senses. Unlike most of my friends, I didn't want a truck or a job or a scholarship; I wanted a horse and a quest and a buried treasure. But there were no real quests anymore. Not in my town. So I had to make them up. And that led to a series of hijinks that I'll write about when I'm old and most of the witnesses are dead and the statute of limitations has run out.

But I left out something significant when I told you about my conversation with Granny Peterson: when she asked me what kind of books I liked to read, the prevailing feeling I remember is bashfulness, just a few inches shy of outright embarrassment. I was standing in her front room with my hand on the table where the grownups always played canasta, and I stared at the linoleum floor, wishing she hadn't asked me that question. Ask me about something else, I thought. Anything else. Skateboarding or girlfriends or grades or Jesus. Leave my stories alone. My craving for those tales occupied a private part of my adolescence; they represented my loneliness, the only antidote for which was the seemingly impossible dream that life could be lived alongside trusty companions and in defiance of great evil.

I looked out her window and saw crabgrass, old trucks, clouds of mosquitoes, and gravel roads, a rural slowth that drawled, "Here's your life, son. Make do." But my books said, "Here's a sword, lad. Get busy." A persistent fear sizzled in my heart, a fear that there existed no real adventure other than the one on the page, and that I was doomed never to know it. Doomed to a life of failure. There's that word again. I felt called to adventure but saw no way to get there, so instead I read about adventures and kept that dream alive by keeping it to myself. How do you explain that to Granny? How, for that matter, do you explain it to anyone?

Sooner or later, I had to abandon the salt lick. I needed water. Sometime between adolescence and my diploma, I discovered music, and music was the horse that bore me safely out of town. Music was the call to adventure, however self-serving and reckless that adventure may have been. It was also the doorway through which the object of my quest entered my heart.

In the summer of 1993 I was a foundering young man chaperoning at a youth conference called CIY (Christ in Youth), when one morning at Milligan College, on a hillside by the chapel, I watched the sun rise on the green mountains. They were more beautiful than any landscape I had imagined existing in Krynn or Prydain or even Middle-earth. They were real mountains. My CD Walkman was on repeat, and again and again I heard Rich Mullins sing the lines, "I see the morning moving over the hills / I can see the shadows on the western side / and all those illusions that I had / they just vanish in your light." The sun was rising on me, pushing the shadows of my failure and fear farther and farther away until the whole world was bright and peaceful as only an Appalachian dawn can be when you're nineteen and weeping with the surety of true forgiveness and true love. What I was looking for all along had found me instead.

Not once did I suspect in all my sketching and reading and aching to enter the stories I read that Jesus was calling to me through them. Jesus was mostly an idea. There was church, the life I was supposed to long for, and then there was the life I actually longed for. You see, I was the victim of what I call *imaginational segregation*. On one hand there was my compulsion to be a Christian—a cultural and familial paradigm that I happily ascribed to and had little reason to resist—and on the other hand I nurtured a mostly secret affection for what were, more or less, fairy tales. Looking back, the same was true of my obsession with comic books and films and music. In each of those art forms I encountered a world that seemed more vivid than the one I was in. I wanted to enter that beauty. And I decided the only way to engage it, apart from my imagination, was to create it. I could draw, or play the piano, or write. If I could make something beautiful, maybe I could forget for a few moments how drab I was, how useless I felt, how lonely was this dull and lifeless life I had been given—and that dull life included Christianity as I understood it. I was, of course, projecting my disappointment with myself onto everything else—everything but the world in my mind, built out of song and story and that terrible, secret longing. The grass was oh-so-much greener on the Other Side. The mountains were taller and the water was sweeter and the stories were better, too.

But that morning when I was nineteen on the hillside in East Tennessee, things were different. Life itself—the one I was actually living—for once outshone the life I had yearned for. The Maker of this beautiful, broken world ambushed me. He had lain in wait for the perfect moment to spring: the perfect song at the perfect hour of the day, the contrition of my hungry heart, the intricate staging of the beauty that had led me to that dewy lawn, and his holy, brooding spirit draped over the valley like a mist. "Drink," he told me, "and thirst no more."

I'm not saying this was my actual conversion, but it was a salient moment that perhaps marked the end of a season of struggle. When the shadows cast by my disappointment and self-hatred were banished by the light of the forgiveness, the acceptance, and the infinite affection of Christ, I could see the world around me for the miracle it was. I could see myself as a miracle. Scripture tells us that when God looks at a Christian he sees Christ's righteousness—in a similar way, the Christian is now free to see Christ in everything. Even himself. I was gloriously alive, and I was at home in the palm of God's hand.

So I abandoned fantasy. I had no need for it, so I thought, because the world I was in pulsed with loveliness. I was wide-awake to God's presence. I cried when I sang in church. That was a new one for me. The Bible became fascinating for the first time since I had read Revelation at church camp to see how imminent was the apocalypse in order to gauge my remaining party time. Now I read it because it felt alive. I read it to know the God Rich Mullins seemed to know so well. And you know what? It worked. During the first few weeks of Bible college the story of the Old Testament lit up my imagination with stories of battle, espionage, love triangles, deception, failure, heroism, and the promise of redemption; mine was an imagination well-prepared for the invasion of the gospel story. The soil had been fertilized in my youth with a hundred tales that had taken root and grown but had born no fruit; those old stories withered, then decayed and composted, readying the ground for the life-giving seeds that were coming.

I feasted on the meat of the Bible for four years. I don't want to give the impression that I was a model student, or that I rejoiced in writing papers on the problem of evil or the kings of Judah. In many ways I was still the bonehead I always was. And yet, I no longer felt that awful lack of purpose, which is, I suppose, a lack of hope. Now there were songs to be written. There were concerts to play. I wanted to tell people this story that had changed me, and through the lens of all my newfound hope, the world and every person I met seemed to shimmer with God's presence. I read commentaries. I read every class syllabus. I read the Bible. I read papers. I was eating meat, meat, meat, and more meat.

Then at the beginning of my senior year, with a bit of leftover student loan money burning a hole in the pocket of my chapel slacks, I accidentally bought *The Chronicles of Narnia* from the college bookstore. I was hunting for the semester's textbooks when I spotted all seven paperbacks in an attractive white slipcase, much like the set I grew up with. I stood in the aisle with an unwieldy stack of textbooks and three-ring binders in one hand, while with the other I experienced a familiar tingle in the tips of my fingers as I ran them over the books that contained the magic of Narnia. I remembered the word I heard that morning on the mountain: "Drink."

The books went home with me, and I showed them to Jamie (to whom I'd been married for about a year). "For our future kids," I said, but that wasn't the whole truth. I had read so much non-fiction in college that I was craving something light and non-required. Somehow, during my last semester of school, even though I was doing a steady stream of concerts and I needed to complete an internship and twenty-two hours of credit to graduate, I managed to read C. S. Lewis's story of Aslan and Narnia for the first time since childhood. I read it all the way from the wardrobe to the last battle. I thought of it as a literary retreat, indulging some of my childhood reading tendencies to give my brain a rest from academia. But instead, I experienced something much deeper.

The reintroduction of fairy tales to my redeemed imagination helped me to see the Maker, his Word, and the abounding human (but sometimes Spirit-commandeered) tales as interconnected. It was like holding the intricate crystal of Scripture up to the light, seeing it lovely and complete, then discovering on the sidewalk a spray of refracted colors. The colors aren't Scripture, nor are they the light behind it. Rather, they're an expression of the truth, born of the light beyond, framed by the prism of revelation, and given expression on solid ground. My final days in college were spent studying the books of Ezekiel and James in class, writing song lyrics in the margins of my syllabi, and reading, at last, *The Lord of the Rings*, that exquisite spray of refracted light.

The point is, Tolkien's story bears many similarities to those I read in high school (mostly due to their imitation of him), including the lure of escapism. In the same way the *Dragonlance* books had whisked me out of high school, Tolkien's books transported me out of college for a few precious minutes each day. But whether it was because of my own awakening to the beauty of life through the saving truth of the gospel or because of Tolkien's own faith and attentiveness to the Holy Spirit while writing *The Lord of the Rings*, when his story ended the world around me held *more* possibility, not less; it was brighter, not duller; my eyes were clearer, not dimmer. Tolkien and Lewis, both in their own way, lifted me out of this world to show me a thundering beauty, and when I read the last sentence and came tumbling back to earth, I could still hear the peal. I hear it to this day.

God allowed the stories to lift the veil on the imaginary world to show me the real world behind it—which ended up being, in the end, the one I was already in. Tolkien and Lewis held the fabric of Narnia or Middle-earth in one hand and clutched ours in the other, building a bridge so we could set out for perilous realms and return safely with some of the beauty we found there. The ache we feel when we read about Frodo's voyage to the Grey Havens, the ache we feel when Lucy hears the thump of solid wood at the back of the wardrobe is telling us that yes, there's another world. But the stories that awaken us are meant to awaken us not only to the reality to come but to this world and its expectant glory. Too often we retreat into the pages of our longing only to return disconsolate to the kitchen or the classroom—we're escaping *from* and not *to*.

A few years ago I dug out a few of the fantasy novels I loved and found them mostly empty. Not only have my tastes changed (the quality of the writing left something to be desired), but they strike me as a way to pass the time rather than enrich it. The accoutrements of fantasy and science fiction still hold their appeal for me; dragons and quests and epic tales are appetizing seasonings, but seasonings don't make a meal. Nowadays I read more broadly—novels that take place not just at Hogwarts but in Iowa (which I have learned is no less magical). I've been enraptured by stories about moths and watermelon harvesting and bridge building, and non-fiction about city planning and hurricanes and explorers of the Amazon. There's so much out there to read that now I'd never answer my grandmother's question with: "Fantasy novels." If someone asked me today, my answer would be, "Good books." The same is true of music: "Good music." Is that a genre?

That doesn't mean I don't have a soft spot for dragons. I believe the Lord used those books to pique my desire for another world, to exercise the muscle of imagination (if not prose), and even to comfort a lonely kid. I'm sure God's doing the same for kids all over the world, even now.

I'm not ashamed to admit that when I go to Barnes & Noble I still visit the fantasy section first. I still run my fingers along the spines and study the cover art. And I still feel that 1987 tingle. Sometimes I even read some of those books. I tell myself it's just for fun, but I'll let you in on a secret: I'm on the hunt. Somewhere out there, there's another Tolkien.

Somewhere out there, men and women with redeemed, integrated imaginations are sitting down to spin a tale that awakens, a tale that leaves the reader with a painful longing that points them home, a tale whose fictional beauty begets beauty in the present world and heralds the world to come. Someone out there is building a bridge so we can slip across to elf-land and smuggle back some of its light into this present darkness.

I'm always looking for that bridge.

I suppose you could call it a quest.

8

THE BLACK BOX

A poet is a man who is glad of something, and tries to make other people glad of it, too."[5] George MacDonald wrote that a hundred years ago. That's one way of looking at songwriting. But a songwriter is also a person who is sad about something and wants other people to be sad about it too, or is confused by something and wants others to feel that confusion. Songwriting is about resonance.

Nikola Tesla, the enigmatic inventor, made this mysterious black box. Legend has it he figured out that every object has a resonant frequency, and by attaching his black box to anything he could find its frequency and increase the intensity by degrees until the thing was vibrating wildly. Imagine a kid on a swing starting at zero, kicking her legs and leaning back, kicking her legs and leaning back. Soon she's swinging for the clouds, right? That's the idea with Tesla's black box. Supposedly he tried it in his lab and found success, then decided to test his black box on a Manhattan high-rise that was under construction. He snuck in after hours, attached his box to an I beam, increased the frequency a bit at a time, and soon the building was trembling so much that the whole thing almost collapsed. I imagine bolts rattling loose and raining down around him in the dark. He detached the box just in time, slipped back to his laboratory, and the next morning

---

5. George MacDonald, *At the Back of the North Wind* (CreateSpace Independent Publishing Platform, 2015).

announced to the press that, given enough time, he could break the planet in two.

I've heard songs that broke my heart in three minutes flat.

If you're reading this, it's a safe assumption that you have at least a passing interest in the creative process—maybe songs, maybe novels, maybe art or poetry or whatever. Having written some novels while in the throes of a decent career as a singer-songwriter, I get this question over and over: "Is there any correlation between the two? How is songwriting different than writing books?" Part of the answer is something Rich Mullins said: songwriting is like going fishing. Sometimes you sit by the pond all day and never catch a thing. But sometimes you snag something beautiful. The point is, you never know unless you go to the pond and wait.

If that analogy is right, and I think there's a lot of truth to it, songwriting is about patience. For me, going to the pond means getting a new composition notebook, sitting with the guitar, and throwing out lines. Most nights I go to bed at 3:00 a.m. with a few ideas scribbled on the page, maybe a melody or a chord progression in my head. The next morning I revisit the work only to discover, quite often, that none of it is any good. No fish. Then it's back to square one. You just keep going to the pond over and over until you catch something worth keeping.

So if songwriting is about patience, writing a book is about endurance. You don't really need that flash of inspiration to write a book. In fact, the whole process is about as mundane as you can imagine, churning out pages made out of paragraphs made out of sentences made out of words. If inspiration comes, you don't really know it until the book is finished. Not only that, the satisfaction of sharing it with someone is deferred for months, if not years.

On the other hand, when I've worked on a song for a few weeks and I think I'm finished, I can play it for someone right away. As I said before, that moment of connection is nothing short of magical, and reminds me that I'm alive. You pour just as much of your heart into a story, though, and the kicker is, nobody's going to read it for a long, long time. You could be not just barking up the wrong tree but hunting in the wrong forest altogether and not know it until you're considerably older. Not only that, even after the book is finished, there's a good chance that a lot of your friends will never read it. Either they're not readers, they're not into the genre, or they just don't have the time. It's best not to ask your friends if they've read your book because the awkward shuffling of feet is unbearable. At first it bugged me, but now I've faced the fact that I haven't read some of my friends' books and it's certainly not because I don't love them. I just haven't gotten to it yet, what with all the stories out there to be read. Also, there's Netflix.

So, songs require patience. Books require endurance. Songs are 100-meter dashes. Books are marathons. You have a lot more opportunity to question your sanity when you're battling your way through the jungle of a novel for a year.

But how are they the same?

They both take work. Different kinds of work, but it's all work.

They both require imagination—"imaging" something in your mind that doesn't yet exist—and also creativity, which is the work of incarnating the idea.

They both require courage. That isn't to say that I'm particularly courageous, but that I'm particularly afraid. Afraid of rejection. Afraid of failure. Afraid of ridicule. Fear is a mighty wind, and some of us merely have a creative spark.

Perhaps most important, they both require revision. And revision usually means collaboration. Whenever I talk to students, one of the key points I try to make is that their teachers aren't crazy or cruel to make them edit and revise their papers. Author Jonathan Rogers gave me that advice on things to talk about at school visits. Not only do the kids need to learn revision, they need to hear from someone else that their teachers are right. The thing the Resistance doesn't want you to know is that revision is the fun part. My brother, an author and playwright, is also a formidable editor. He understands story as well as anyone I know, and he delights in revision.

Once he told me that the hard part is finding the clay, the raw material of the story. It takes work to harvest clay. You have to go to a stream and grab a bucket of mud, mix it with water, sift out the rougher sediment, pour off the water, allow the moisture to seep through a cloth for days. That's your first draft. After that you get to flop the clay onto the pottery wheel and turn it into something better than mud, hopefully something both useful and beautiful. That's revision. Whether you're writing a song or a story, you have to shape it and reshape it, scrap it and start over, always working it as close as it can get to the thing it wants to become. But first you need that muddy lump, the first draft.

After that, when the shaping begins, how do you know if you're on the right track? You share it with someone. (Again, courage is a requirement.) But not just anyone. Share it with a better writer than you. Share it with someone who'll be careful with you, who will tell you the truth in love. Sometimes you'll thank them kindly and ignore them completely because what do they know, anyway? Other times they'll confirm your worst suspicions, because you knew all along that something wasn't working, but, let's face it again, you were being lazy. You just wanted to be done. That's the cancer. That's the nest of roaches you have to exterminate from your story. Roll up your sleeves and kill them dead, because the world has enough bad stories. Nobody said it would be easy.

A few practical considerations, now that I'm on a writing soapbox. Over the years I've taught a number of writing classes, with varying success. Whenever the invitation includes the word *workshop*, I balk. I don't really want to teach a workshop if it means critiquing or facilitating the critique of someone's work. Now, I'm not saying that workshops have no value. I'm sure there are really helpful ones out there, and for some people that fellowship with others working to hone their craft is indispensable. Go for it. But it sounds miserable to me—on both sides of the coin. Heads, I'm sitting in a room where people are passing judgment on a fledgling piece of my work; tails, I'm the leader, trying to think of something good to say about someone's weak paragraph, when what I want to tell them is that they should just keep writing and reading, reading and writing.

I know, I know. I'm a terrible person. The better angels of my nature tell me to encourage, to offer sage advice, to create a nurturing environment, because Lord knows I've received that kind of help over the years.

So when I teach, I try to offer a handful of principles that I believe are helpful for cultivating a writing life, principles that can be applied broadly to several disciplines. See, I don't think the artist's life should be exclusive to artists. People who make their living in the arts aren't any more interesting than everybody else. I used to think, arrogantly, that once I was a Real Author or a Professional Musician, people would be impressed. I'm here to tell you they really, really aren't—not for long, at least. Hearing your own song on the radio is one of the coolest experiences in the world, and so is seeing your book on the shelf at Barnes and Noble. But after the thrill fades, you're still just plain old you.

That just reminded me of a story I've only told my wife.

A few years back I was in a Barnes & Noble somewhere far away from where I live. I had finished my browsing and was about to leave, when I heard my name. Someone at the information desk at the center of the store was asking an employee where they might find books by Andrew Peterson. There are a couple of other authors by that name, so I figured they were asking about the academic Andrew, or the special-ops thriller Andrew—surely not the fantasy author Andrew. "His first book is called On the Edge of the Dark Sea of Darkness," the customer said. Please understand how odd this was for me. To be in a random city, at a random bookstore, and hear a random person asking for my book out of the forty thousand books in that store, was so coincidental that it made me think one of two things was happening: either I was being pranked or God had some great lesson for me. Maybe both.

I sheepishly approached the counter and introduced myself, certain that these people would be as gobsmacked by the coincidence as I was.

"I don't think they have my books in stock at this store," I said, "but you can order them online easily enough."

"Oh, thanks!" the person said kindly. "I've heard the books are good and wanted to get one for my niece." Then they went back to browsing, utterly unsurprised and unimpressed. I might as well have been another employee. Between you and me, is that weird? It's weird, right? I mean, how many times have you been looking for a book and had the author appear at your shoulder to help you?

The point is, that's an extreme example of what happens all the time with books and music. People think it's cool and they're usually very kind, but the thrill fades so quickly for both me and them that it's more like bumping into your plumber at the grocery store than meeting an actual famous person. And that's exactly as it should be.

Back to what I was saying. Hearing your song on the radio and seeing your book in a bookstore are truly delightful experiences. But other than those quick affirmations that your work is reaching people, the daily grind isn't much different from anyone else. So being a writer is more like being an architect or a soldier or a nurse than most people realize. It's a craft that you're constantly learning, a craft that is shaped by a bit of talent in submission to a great deal of work. So when I teach about writing, my hope is that the principles are cross-disciplinary and will enrich more than just your area of interest. If you're a writer, cultivating these principles may not lead to a good living, but they can lead to a good life.

You won't end up with a black box that will break the earth in half, but the steady resonance of your work might move someone closer to the Kingdom—and compared to a human heart, planets are small potatoes.

9

SERVING THE WORK

If you've never read Madeline L'Engle's *Walking on Water*, put
down this book and don't come back to it until you have. This
is a courageous thing for me to say, because once you've read
her book there's not much point in reading this one.

I first read it not long after I had moved to Nashville,
when I was struggling to articulate my vocation to myself or
to anyone else. Among the many wonderful things she covers,
she talks about "serving the work."

The creative process is a profound mystery. I love hearing
authors and artists try and explain where their ideas come
from. Whether they believe in God or not, there's always a tone
of reverence, surprise, or even befuddlement when they talk
about it. More often than not, there are a few common threads.
One is that the thing came to them along the way, which is to
say the real flash of inspiration came not before they started
working, but during the process. Another common thread is
that the story or song seems to have a will of its own.

I remember hearing a lot about that before I started
writing my first book and was creeped out, to be honest. I
was doubtful it would happen to me, but hoped it would, in
the same way I hope to see a ghost when I'm in an old house.
But artists often have a sense that their story, song, painting,
or sculpture "wants" to become something, often something
quite different from what they intended.

Sounds strange, I know, but it couldn't be more true to
my experience. It's like there's a platonic form of the song out

there somewhere, and you get a tiny glimpse of that true form at some stage in the creative act. Half the job is fighting to get the feeble work of your hands as close as possible to that flash of beauty. You have the sense that you aren't the one who conceived of the thing but are a surrogate mother helping to birth something new into the world. That doesn't mean we turn off our brains, or that we forfeit our agency in shaping the art. There's a paradox at work here. Serving the work doesn't mean we don't have an agenda, but that the agenda works in partnership with the wild, creative spirit—not as an overlord.

One great problem with much art that's called "Christian" is agenda, which is to say that it's either didactic, or manipulative, or merely pragmatic—in other words, the artistic purity of the work tends to take a back seat to the artist's agenda. L'Engle says art that isn't good is, by definition, not Christian art, while on the other hand art that's good, true, and beautiful *is* Christian art, no matter what the artist believes. If you have problems with that assertion, like I said, read *Walking on Water*. (You were supposed to go read it before you got to this page, come to think of it, right?) L'Engle makes a compelling argument, and I happen to agree—for the most part.

I'm going to say something that might not be very cool here, so prepare yourself. Art and agenda can and do coexist. Having an agenda isn't necessarily a bad thing. In fact, some of history's greatest works of art are dripping with agenda. If you've ever walked into a cathedral in Europe, you've walked into a monumental agenda. The architects weren't just making beauty for beauty's sake. They were (some of them, at least) striving to bring glory to God, building a three-dimensional story for us to walk into, one designed for very specific reasons (to create a feeling of mystery and smallness in us, to draw attention to the cross of Jesus, to pull our eyes upward toward light and glory, to retell the story of Scripture through paintings and stained glass). The fact that these architects and artists had an agenda doesn't at all reduce the power of what they made. Agenda isn't necessarily bad. Even someone who doesn't believe a word of the Bible walks into the Notre Dame Cathedral and falls silent. But a Christian familiar with the symbolism, the narrative, not to mention the actual Triune God the cathedral was made for, is just as awestruck at the beauty but *also* gets the truth thrown in with it.

Agenda is bad when it usurps the beauty. Christian art should strive for a marriage of the two, just as Christ is described as being "full of grace and truth" (John 1:14). Truth without beauty can be a weapon; beauty without truth can be spineless. The two together are like lyric and melody. This is not to say that beauty itself isn't a kind of truth, nor that truth itself isn't beautiful. It'll take a better philosopher than me to parse all that out. (I commend to you authors like Steve Guthrie and Jeremy Begbie if you want to swim in those deep but lovely waters.) Hopefully, though, you see my point. There's a purist approach to art in which the artist is expected to create simply for the sake of creating, making beauty for its own sake; the artist operates with abandon and is loathe to interfere or try and control the wild impulse of art. It does have a certain romance. But we're not merely artistic, creative creatures—we're rational, articulate creatures, too, so why not bring both to bear?

For a Christian, depending on your calling, this means not cowering from the idea that you're writing your story with a certain set of beliefs on full display, or from the secret hope that your work will accomplish some very specific things, like bringing attention to the gospel, or waking up a yearning for God himself in someone's heart, or conveying in a compelling way something you believe to be true. Christian art, then, might be defined as a work that is, like Christ himself, full of grace *and* truth.

Where we go wrong is when we tilt the scales away from grace, or beauty, or excellence, as if truth were all that mattered. When you look at a Rembrandt or read a Tolkien, you're getting lyric and melody, truth and beauty. The beauty, by its excellence, bears the truth to the world in a way that seasons culture and can arrest the attention of the staunchest atheist. This is where I wonder about L'Engle's definition of Christian art. I think there's truly great art that isn't Christian because, while Beethoven's "Moonlight Sonata" is one of the most beautiful piano pieces in the world, it doesn't articulate anything about the gospel. It may be the music that God uses to ambush someone with *sehnsucht*, but he can use a smile from a stranger or even a flower for that and that doesn't make it a Christian flower. Let me be clear, I'm not suggesting that there's not inherent value in non-explicit art—just that it might be an oversimplification to define it as "Christian" art.

When I moved to Nashville it was cool to say that I wasn't a Christian artist, but an artist who was a Christian. That's not necessarily a bad thing, but the measure of potential snootiness in that statement is an indication of its incompleteness.

The fact is, there's nothing wrong with being a Christian artist. Fanny Crosby, I would argue, was a Christian artist. Bach was a Christian artist. Rich Mullins was a Christian artist. Michaelangelo, in some measure, was a Christian artist. Their calling was to make art specifically for or about the church, explicitly, at times, about the person of Jesus Christ. That, from a standpoint of vocation, is different from, say, the Christian called to write pop songs or love songs, or mystery writers like P. D. James or Dorothy Sayers, who were masters of the craft but would never have described themselves as Christian mystery writers. Theirs was a subtler calling, making them able to influence culture with truths, or, in the case of mainstream musicians, to move comfortably in their arenas in a way that someone like Fanny Crosby or even C. S. Lewis couldn't.

Again, I'm not arguing here that one is better than another—just that there is, in fact, a difference. There's a difference in calling, in audience, in execution, in content. And those on either side of the coin should celebrate the calling in one another, because the fact is, God is going to speak through the arts no matter who's making it—which is what L'Engle, I think, was getting at.

After twenty years of making music for a living, I've finally come to the conclusion that I'm a Christian who is an artist, who usually tries to make Christian art (according to my above definition). Whenever I'm at a Paul Simon or James Taylor concert there's a part of me that wonders what my career would have looked like if I had pursued something in the mainstream. It sure looks fun, what with the crowds so delightfully uninhib-ited—unlike my typical church audience, who never dance, and aren't exactly rowdy.[6] But then I consider my calling. My calling, as best as I can tell, came around the time I was nineteen and had fallen in love with Jesus by way of the music of Rich Mullins. I asked God to let me use my gifts for his Kingdom, and if it was his will, to let me bless other people in the way that Rich's songs had blessed me. That meant not shying away from any tendency to talk about the reality of Jesus' work in my life. It meant finding ways to bring the Bible to life in lyrics. It meant telling stories about my heart—its desolation by sin and its renewal by grace. But part of that calling also meant aspiring to writing with the same kind of excellence that Rich Mullins wrote with. It wasn't just a call to write about Jesus. It was a call to try to write *beautifully* about him.

A caveat: I realize that I'm walking a tightrope here. It would be the height of arrogance to get cocky about any

---

6. I'm not trying to guilt anybody, but I'm going to take this moment to provide a little Public Service Announcement on behalf of my singer-songwriter friends who usually play in churches: dear audience, we need you. A concert is best when it's a two-way street. We don't want you to clap and shout because we're arrogant, but because we're human and need your encouragement. It's not easy to stand on a stage and bare your soul to a room of strangers, especially when that room is mostly empty and you feel like a giant failure, so when a song is over, remember that you have a great deal of power to bless the people on stage with a heap of love and kindness, just by clapping joyfully as soon as the song is over and not after two seconds of awkward silence, during which time the artist dies a thousand deaths. Have you ever been to a Springsteen concert? It's an incredible experience, and he completely pours himself out because the audience is drinking it up. If you want to see your favorite performers at their best, love them well from your seat.

excellence in my own songs, so let me be clear. I think I'm a good songwriter. I have a gift, and have had some success at it. But I don't for a second think that I'm a *great* songwriter, not like Rich, or Paul Simon, or James Taylor (a quick look at record sales would substantiate this claim), or about fifteen of my songwriter friends in Nashville. So please don't read into this that I think I'm awesome. As soon as my sinful heart goes there all I have to do is remember Rich's "The Color Green" or James Taylor's "Copperline" or Paul Simon's "American Tune" or Andy Gullahorn's "Grand Canyon" or Ben Shive's "EGBDF," and I remember how much I have to learn.

The point is, I had no interest in cheesing out to write Christian music. The very thing about Rich Mullins that got my attention was the poetry, the imagery, the lyrical dexterity so evident in his songs. *That* was what I asked God for. There were other people doing the other kind of Christian music. I wanted to learn how to do that one thing, which was to sing about the winds of heaven *and* the stuff of earth. Folk songs, story songs, gritty songs—but also songs that were unabashedly about this wonderful, heartbreaking, confusing life as a Christian.

All that sounds great, but I had no idea how to do it. There were plenty of times that I copped out and wrote a song that was dripping with Scripture and truth, thinking that would be enough. But it wasn't. There was no craft, no real heart behind it.

And there were times when I bled all over the audience and dressed up my opinions in meter and rhyme, thinking *that* would be enough. But it wasn't.

Over the years when life started really beating me up and I was forced to dig deeper than opinions and work harder than panning Scripture for gold nuggets that might make a good song, I began to understand the peril of asking God to let you write songs that would comfort the lonely and broken-hearted—peril, because the only way to do that is to walk through the dark forest of loneliness and heartbreak.

I had to learn that when you're writing a song, you have to *serve the work*. You have to remember that the God the song is about knows more than you do about songwriting. Your agenda should be broad: "Let this song be a light in someone's darkness. Let this song bring you glory, Father. Use it to lead someone home." Then let the song suggest itself to you. Discover it. Fumble around in the dark room, feeling for the shape of it. Don't use your agenda to bully it into being. And when you realize it wants to go somewhere you didn't intend, · *let it*. Be willing to trash the rest of the song (or the essay, or the painting, or the screenplay, or the sermon) if you have to in order to find the thing it wants to be. *That's* when agenda is bad. When you cast all mystery out the window because you want to make a point, you're in essence declaring yourself the master and not the servant. Be humble. The creative act is profoundly spiritual, and therefore profoundly mysterious. It's like in *Indiana Jones and the Last Crusade*, when Indy says, "The penitent man shall pass," and realizes at the last moment that if he doesn't duck he's going to lose his head, only in this case you won't lose your head, you'll lose the song. Bow to the Lord of music, ask him to help you make the song what it's supposed to be—not what *you* want it to be. Drink from that well, then maybe you'll have some water to give to the thirsty.

It goes without saying (I hope) that since God is always inviting us frail humans into the creative process, that doesn't mean we check our taste at the door and write garbage. We're not zombies, nor should we be presumptuous about what the song wants to be. Humility means working that much harder to make it beautiful.

On the Steven Curtis Chapman tour in 2011, I was desperate to write songs. I knew we would be hitting the studio in a matter of weeks, and I didn't have a single new song written. Being the opener on a tour is a great opportunity to write because of the abundance of free time. Not only that, it's inspiring to be rubbing elbows with other songwriters and musicians. I remember hearing Billy Joel say once that when he faces writer's block he puts on a tweed jacket, brings a notebook to a smoky bar in New York, sits in a corner and *pretends* like he's a songwriter; sometimes it's enough to convince himself. There's something to be said for that, especially when you're susceptible to certain voices in your head. It reminds me of George MacDonald's admonition to know God by obeying him. If you want to know the mind of God, do what he says. Jesus, who knew the Father completely, also obeyed the Father completely. Similarly (though I know it's a stretch), if you want to know what it's like to be a songwriter, put on your tweed and write a song. It's as simple and as difficult as that.

Back to the tour. Every time I found a few hours of free time I ducked into a choir room or Sunday school classroom with my guitar and tried to find a song. By the middle of the tour I had finished one and started about seven, but I was on the hunt for more. Then one day in soundcheck, a song dropped out of the sky. Ben Shive started playing this really cool piano part, then Ken Lewis started drumming to it, and in moments everyone in the room stopped what they were doing. The rest of the band hurried over to their instruments and without a word started playing along. Brent Milligan put on his bass. Josh Wilson and I started strumming. Harold Rubens at the soundboard stopped tweaking and started listening. Something cool was happening.

If you're a musician or a songwriter, chances are you know what I'm talking about. I'm not usually one for jamming, but sometimes someone discovers a chord progression or a melody or a rhythm that's like a magic key. It opens a door to a wide field of inspiration and beauty. It's a rare occurrence, and I imagine it feels quite a bit like the Holy Spirit descending on the house, and we're suddenly speaking the tongues of men and angels.

Lest you think I'm claiming that something I've written is *that* kind of inspired, let me make another disclaimer. First of all, who knows? God can do what he wants, with whomever he wants. But the song as it's written is *never* as beautiful as it was in that fleeting, exhilarating moment of inspiration. The song's potential is shimmering beyond the veil somewhere, while the song that you finally write is almost always haunted by a feeling of diminishment. You have a picture in your mind or a feeling in your heart that you're trying to bring into space and time, but there's just no way (yet) to deliver it in its fullness. The song in reality is as different from what you imagined as a portrait is from the painter's subject. At some point (usually thanks to the mercy of a deadline), you have to put down the brush and give thanks for the chance to have made an attempt.

This has caused me some grief, and a lot of frustration. There are songs on my older albums (I won't tell you which) that I had dreams about, but even as we recorded them I could feel the magic fading. It was like trying to shave as the battery in my Norelco died a slow death and left me half-whiskery. The songwriting process is about trying to find the words and melodies that will get as close as possible to the summit of the mountain first glimpsed through the clouds. Most often, I'm nowhere close. I end up in the desert somewhere, turning the map this way and that. But sometimes I end up at least in the foothills, and go to bed happy; I haven't summited, but I can at least see the peak and imagine what it would be like to stand there.

Those are a few of the thoughts that went through my noggin as we vamped Ben's chord progression. Over the mic I asked Harold at the soundboard to record what we were doing, and he gave me a thumbs-up; he didn't say a word because he didn't want to break the spell. Right away, for reasons I don't know, I thought of Cormac McCarthy's book *The Road*. It's an amazing (and amazingly dark) book about a father and son trying to survive the end of the world. They're traversing the wasteland of America with hunger at their heels and man-eating wretches on their heels, too, trying to reach the ocean where the father believes they'll find help. Along the way, he tells his little boy again and again that they have to "carry the fire." It's a simple, beautiful metaphor that can mean quite a few things. I started singing that phrase during soundcheck, and pretty quickly staked my claim on Ben's piano part by asking if I could write something to it.

It was about a month later that I finally managed to write the verses. They came after a long, hard conversation with a dear friend whose marriage was foundering. He wept, and I ran out of words. I finally tried to put down in a song what I wanted to say to encourage him, and came up with this:

> I will hold your hand, love
> As long as I can, love
> Though the powers rise against us
>
> Though your fears assail you
> And your body may fail you
> There's a fire that burns within us
>
> And we dream in the night
> Of a city descending
> With the sun in the center
> And a peace unending
>
> I will, I will carry the fire
> I will, I will carry the fire
> Carry the fire for you
>
> And we kneel in the water
> The sons and the daughters
> And we hold our hearts before us

And we look to the distance
And raise our resistance
In the face of the forces
Gathered against us

And we dream in the night
Of a King and a kingdom
Where joy writes the songs
And the innocent sing them

I will carry the fire for you

And we dream in the night
Of a feast and a wedding
And the Groom in his glory
When the bride is made ready

I will carry the fire for you

So you see, sometimes a post-apocalyptic literary thriller, plus a cool piano part by your friend in soundcheck, plus an urge to encourage someone going through a divorce can braid together into a song about longing for the Second Coming. But only if you allow the song to lead you.

———————

Someone once asked about getting too comfortable with formulae or song structures, as opposed to (I assume) pushing yourself into unfamiliar territory. I think this is where exercising good old-fashioned discernment is the thing. If you're a lover of good songs, and a student of good songwriting, you'll learn how and when to break the rules. There are conventions we all recognize, and most popular songs these days fall into some version of that. It's not a bad place to start, and it's a tried-and-true way to structure a song. But you also have to be willing to follow your nose. You have to be willing to let the song go where it wants. I think that's the best question to ask when you come to a writing crossroads: "Where does the story want to go?"

Once I got home from a weekend of touring and my daughter Skye, nine at the time, had written me a song. It was a sweet, sad song about how she misses me when I'm gone, complete with a verse, a chorus, another verse, a chorus, and a pretty hook of a la-la-la melody. She's pretty brilliant, and was already saying things like, "I *was* going to do another chorus, but the la-la-la felt better there." She was too young to care too much about song structures, or to feel pressure to conform to the confines of a radio single, or to get hung up on the coherence of an idea. She just sat down at the piano with an emotion and tried to fashion it into a song, without self-consciousness or hubris—just freedom. It's a great reminder to me of how best to approach the process. The Kingdom belongs to such as these.

The way to push yourself into new territory isn't about pushing yourself as much as it is allowing yourself to be pulled along. A few years ago I was talking with Sally Lloyd-Jones, and she described the way she felt going into her new project: "I feel like I'm following clues."

Exactly.

10

SERVING THE AUDIENCE

O kay, I'll give you either *striven* or *raiment*," Ben told me with a chuckle and a well-deserved roll of the eyes, "You can't have both."

He's produced several of my records, and I trust him. We were working on a song called "Hosanna." The second verse opened with the line, "I have striven to remove this raiment, tried to hide every shimmering strand."

In this instance I was more interested in showing off than in caring about the listener. I was geeking out about language, saying in essence, "Behold, listener, what fancy words I hath employed!" Now, there's nothing wrong with using an unusual word in a song from time to time, and it's actually quite nice to see someone work hard to make the rhymes interesting. But there comes a point when it's distracting, and the listener (at best) stops thinking about the song and starts thinking about what a smart cookie the writer must be, or (at worst) doesn't know the word and actually feels dumb. So I had to choose either striven or raiment. I went with, "I have *struggled* to remove this raiment," mainly because *raiment* and *angels* in the next line had a nice slant rhyme. Thank you, Ben, for saving me from myself.

Always, always remember to love the listener. One of my pet peeves is when performers don't accept applause. It's a principle I learned back in the rock band I was in after high school. (More about that some other time.) The management drilled into our heads that after the last big note of each song we had to literally hold out our hands as if to say, "What did you think? Awesome, right?" We were like gymnasts at the Olympics, striking a pose at the end of a routine and waiting for the not-so-thunderous applause. And if the audience did actually enjoy the song, then we had to acknowledge it. It was, they taught us, a matter of gratitude. The people in the bleachers don't *have* to be there, after all. They're giving you money, but the more surprising thing is that they're giving you their *attention*—which is an act of profound generosity in a culture that clamors for every second of our attention already. The very least you can do when they clap after your song is to smile, nod, and say thank you. Don't, whatever you do, for the love of all that is sacred, just tune your guitar while they clap, or turn around and say something to the drummer without acknowledging the grace they're giving you. Each applause is like a bouquet of flowers. Don't be a jerk and toss them on the floor. Say thank you. Mean it.

And that leads me to another opinion, much less strongly held, and one I don't strictly keep to. This is mostly for entertainers, but I think there's a broader principle at work that applies to everyone: when you're playing live, end the song in a way that signals to the audience that it is, in fact, over. End on the root chord of the song, or at least with enough of a flourish to make it obvious. It's a simple matter of hospitality.

I read an article about Yo-Yo Ma's struggle with stage fright, in which he explained that he overcame it by imagining the concert as a dinner party that he was hosting. He noticed that whenever he had a party at his house he was never nervous because he knew he was the host. He was there to serve his guests. So if he treated his concert like a dinner party, he knew his role, which was in many ways to make his guests feel at ease.

To love and serve in the context of a concert means taking charge of the two hours you have with the audience, guiding them somewhere gently, thinking of their needs more than your own, and serving your songs to them as if each one was a course in a meal you had prepared in order to love and honor your guests. So when a song is over, make it clear, for the audience's sake, that it's over. You've said what you want to say, and now it's their turn to talk (i.e., applause). Ending a song without resolution might work great on a record, but when you're performing live and the last chord is a dangling question mark, there's an unnecessary awkwardness before the audience reacts. They'll figure it out, of course, but why make things weird when you don't have to? Just end on the one, the root chord. And then, assuming they clap, *thank them.* Be a good host.

When you're writing a song, or preaching a sermon, or writing a novel, you're still the host. If you want to communicate an idea, pique some longing or joy or gratitude in the listener, then consider your words. Don't show off. Don't use esoteric language unless it's there for a reason. Don't sacrifice the song's effect on the altar of your ego. Jason Gray, one of the most hospitable communicators I know, read somewhere about a kid who loved going on those glass-bottom boat tours in Florida. The boy would lie on his belly, cup his hands around his face and lose himself in the otherworldliness of the river, watching colorful fish float among the reeds in slow motion.

He imagined that he *was* one of the fish. But then sometimes his glasses would slide off his face and clatter onto the thick glass—a jarring reminder that he was just a kid on a boat. The spell would be broken.

A song is like a spell. You learn to say it exactly right, inflect the words just so, play the thing at the perfect tempo, and then sometimes you're truly wielding a mysterious power. The spell can then be repeated by others. You don't even have to be there. By God's grace, a good song can inject beauty into some unsuspecting passerby and lead them to the truth. At a concert you can see it happen: people holding still as statues, arrested by the chord progression, the musical hook, the unfolding of a story or idea, the slight modifications to each verse or chorus to keep their attention. Something as real as a tectonic shift may be happening in their magnificent souls, like the mechanism of a primal clock ticking closer and closer to the triumphant sounding of the bell in the tower, a revelation, a scattering of birds that gives them an apocalyptic glimpse of something more, something lofty and grand that reminds them how small they are, or perhaps something miniscule and profoundly intricate that reminds them of the grand mystery of their selfhood. The song is a tightrope, and the listener is inching along, enraptured by the hope and light raveling in the middle distance. Don't, for goodness sake, distract them. Hold your breath. They're lost in another world, peeking through the fur coats at the wintry glory of Lantern Waste. They're holding still while a butterfly lights on an outstretched forearm. When that happens, the world falls away and you're both a channel for and a recipient of grace.

That's what it means to serve the work and to serve the listener. Proceed with utmost care. Whatever you do, don't let their glasses fall off. Don't break the spell.

———

"Write it like you would say it."

I can't tell you how many times over the years that maxim has snapped me out of whatever florid garbage I was writing. It's a good idea to emulate your heroes, to ask yourself when you get to the bridge, "What would Paul Simon do?" Or when you're writing a sermon, "What would Spurgeon do?" Or when you happen upon a guitar part which, miracle of miracles, sounds unique enough to try and build a song upon, to ask, "How does James Taylor get into a part like this?" Steal boldly, I say.

But most often, when I'm scribbling in a notebook the nonsense that I hope will become a not-unbearable song, when it's late and I'm sleepy and I'm stuck, stuck, stuck, I remember those words: "Write it like you would say it." It usually opens the door to the lyric I was looking for. It keeps me from putting on airs, which we're all prone to do. People can spot a fake a mile away. It's the difference between reading a speech from a podium and looking someone in the eye and telling them, "I love you." It communicates to the listener that you're not pulling any punches but you're not blocking any either. "Trust me," it says. "This might hurt, but if we make it out alive we'll be better for it."

If I had to name one bit of advice that has brought me back to center more than any other, it would be that. "Write it like you would say it." Who gave me that advice? Andy Gullahorn. And on each of his albums he provides example after example of honest, excellent songwriting that always invites me in to a face-to-face conversation that leads to something genuine and healing.

Sometimes it's Andy's humor. I've seen a lot of concerts over the years but I've never, ever seen anyone else make the room laugh merely at the word *Hello*. Ben Shive and I would always look at one another in wonder when, yet again, the crowd chuckled at Andy's greeting, whether we were in Sweden or Connecticut or Texas. The Gullahorn Hello, apparently, is a universal language. And few things delight me like sitting on the side stage and watching the crowd react to a song like "I Haven't Either." *They have no idea what's coming*, I think. And then I realize that, though I've heard the song hundreds of times, it's still doing its work on me too. Tears spring to my eyes, conviction comes quick on the heels of my laughter. It's one of the best working examples I know of C. S. Lewis's principle of sneaking past "watchful dragons." Lewis wrote in an essay called "Sometimes Fairy Stories May Say Best What's to be Said,"

> I thought I saw how stories of this kind could steal past a certain inhibition which had para-lysed much of my own religion in childhood. Why did one find it so hard to feel as one was told one ought to feel about God or the suffer-ings of Christ? I thought the chief reason was that one was told one ought to. An obligation

to feel can freeze feelings. And reverence itself did harm. The whole subject was associated with lowered voices; almost as if it were something medical. But supposing that by casting all these things into an imaginary world, stripping them of their stained-glass and Sunday School associations, one could make them for the first time appear in their real potency? Could one not thus steal past those watchful dragons? I thought one could.[7]

Enter Andy Gullahorn, stripping away the audience's self-righteousness or shame or expectation that they were going to have to listen to a bunch of uptight, guilt-ridden Christians blubbering about Jesus. Instead they get a song about skinny jeans. Or about country music, or shopping malls. *I could hang out with this guy*, they think. And then, gently, lovingly, Gully slips past their watchful dragons and surprises them with a moment of grace. Not judgment, not highfalutin Bible talk. Just an honest conversation. That grace may bring conviction for the self-righteous, or it may be a gentle assurance to the lowly sinner that, despite their worst fears there is a great and graceful Person in the world who loves them as they are and not as they should be. I find myself on both sides of the coin from one minute to the next. Amazingly, both can happen at

7. https://www.nytimes.com/1956/11/18/archives/sometimes-fairy-stories-may-say-best-whats-to-be-said.html

the same time, to the same person, when they're listening to an Andy Gullahorn song.

I've seen, firsthand, the effect of his songs on people in the audience, and it reawakens my wonder at the power of songs as an art form. Three or four minutes, a few chords, a few words—and then in a moment, in the twinkling of an eye, a heart is changed. At the very least, in a world where we walk around numb as lepers so much of the time, a song can make you actually *feel* something, a tingle in a place you thought long dead. That's what the best songs—the best works of art—do for me.

So when I sit down to write a song I often ask myself, as I have for years, what my songwriting heroes would do. That list includes Andy Gullahorn, reminding me to have the guts to write it like I would say it. It's a principle that's simple and yet packed with meaning, just like his songs. It's not just advice for songwriting, though; it's a good way to live. Dash all pretense; be who you are; kick down the walls; love the listener. It's scary, sure. But good songwriting is a call to courage, on both sides of the exchange.

Another example from my own writing. When we were recording *Light for the Lost Boy* I had the basic piano part for what became "You'll Find Your Way." I wanted to write the song for my son Asher, who had just turned thirteen. After several false starts on verses that were broad and unnecessarily poetic, Gully suggested that I simply write it like I would say it. His point was this: don't get philosophical. Don't write the song for everybody. Just pretend like you're talking. Pretend you're looking him in the eye and opening your heart to your little boy. Try to forget that you're writing a song and focus on the kid in front of you.

That night I sat at my piano with tears in my eyes and wrote, "When I look at you, boy, I can see the road that lies ahead. I can see the love and the sorrow." The song opened itself up to me, and whether or not you like how it turned out, I managed to write it in a way that my thirteen-year-old kid could receive it as love from his papa.

11

SELECTIVITY

Whenever I get demos from young songwriters, there's usually one glaring problem: the songs are too long. Don't worry, it happens to the best of us. Back in the day I did a string of shows with Mitch McVicker, the protégé of Rich Mullins, and I remember playing him a new song. He was very kind, and very kindly said, "You always use pre-choruses. Why do you do that?"

I'm sure I got defensive, arguing about artistic integrity and all that jazz, but the next time I sat down to write a song you'd better believe it was on my radar. Did I really need all those pre-choruses? Were they saying the same thing every time? Did they move the song forward, or did the listener get restless? What was the point, other than me liking to hear myself talk? Or did I assume the listener wasn't smart enough to get the chorus without my help? (I realize some of this might seem opposed to all the servanthood stuff in the last chapter, but go with it.) Now, a pre-chorus isn't a bad thing. You just need to be able to discern what's necessary to the aesthetic of the song and what isn't. Then lose what isn't.

Here's the lyric for my song "Nothing to Say," which I wrote back in 1995.

> Hey Jamie, would you mind
> Driving down this road awhile?
> Arizona's waiting on these eyes

Rich is on the radio,
And I think we ought to take it slow
Arizona's caught me by surprise

Hey Jamie, have you heard
A picture paints a thousand words
But the photographs don't tell it all

I see the eagle swim the canyon sea
Creation yawns in front of me
Oh Lord, I never felt so small

And now the pre-chorus:

And I don't believe
That I believed in you
As deeply as today
I reckon what I'm saying
Is there's nothing more,
nothing more to say

Then, at last, we get to the chorus:

And the mountains sing your glory hallelujah
The canyons echo sweet amazing grace
My spirit sails, the mighty gales
Are bellowing your name
And I've got nothing to say
I've got nothing to say

During the pre-production meetings with the producer, he kept hacking away at the lyric, asking, "Can we shorten up this turnaround? Can we do only one of those verses? Can we maybe *not* repeat the pre-chorus?" But my boxing gloves were on. How dare he presume to alter my artistic vision? How dare he suggest that my precious songs needed to be shorter? Because he's a good producer, he knew how to trick me. He would say, "Let's just try it this way, and if you don't like it in a few days we can go back." Every single time, he turned out to be right. Which is a nice way of saying that every single time, I was wrong. In the original version of "Nothing to Say," there was another pre-chorus between those first two verses, which meant that we didn't get to the chorus for about 90 seconds. Now when I play the song live, I can't imagine it the old way.

One more quick example from the same record. I wrote "All the Way Home" back in 1994, I think, and it's about my maternal grandparents, who homesteaded a dairy farm in South Florida. The song meant a lot to me, and I was precious about every single line. From the beginning I knew it was long, but I didn't care. I fought the producer over this one hard enough that I eventually won and he let the song stand as it was written. But about ten years later, once my Selectivity Monitor was in better shape, I began to sense the audience's restlessness after the bridge, before the final pre-chorus *then* the final chorus. Once again, did I really need the pre-chorus to set up the final stretch? (Mitch McVicker's words were ringing truer and truer by this point, so if I was going to cut something it was definitely going to be the pre-chorus.)

Fast-forward to 2016, twenty-two years later. I did a run of shows with my children as the band and "All the Way Home" was one of our songs. I finally cut the last pre-chorus, shortening it from the recorded version, and do you know what? Not only did I like the song better, not one single person who was familiar with the original ever noticed, or if they did, they never said so. The lesson is, after your song is finished look at the lyric. Play it live several times. Then if there's anything in the song that no one would notice was missing, axe it *now*. Don't wait two decades. After a while you'll learn the art of selectivity and you'll anticipate those superfluous moments and pull the weeds before they choke the flowers.

I can hear you thinking, "But what's wrong with letting a song stretch its legs?" Nothing, as long as the song is good enough to justify it. As you grow as a writer, you'll figure out what needs to be said and what doesn't, and you'll know when to let it breathe. Some plants need pruning. Others are meant to grow wild.

The other reason young songwriters's songs are too long is that their songs are about five things instead of one. We can be so pleased with our ingenuity, our expansive poetry, that we think each song needs to be epic. That's just not true.

Anne Lamott, in her wonderful book *Bird by Bird* (one of the few books about writing that I recommend every chance I get) tells about a writing exercise she gave her students. I haven't read it in a while, but here's how I remember it. They were to choose an old family photo, put a one-inch picture frame over part of it, and then write about only what's in that little square. Don't write about Uncle Clarence if he's not in there. Maybe write about his shoulder there in the corner, but focus on the blurry painting on the wall in the background, or Aunt Gertrude's pearl earring. Lamott's point is that you can fill pages and pages with what's in that tiny space. One thought leads to another, leads to another, leads to another, and when that string runs out you can return to the one-inch frame and find another telling element to get you running.

Anytime someone says they don't know what to write about, I think of this exercise. The trouble isn't that there isn't anything to write about; the trouble is that there's too much. Boiling all those brilliant thoughts kicking around in your brilliant brain is tough work, to be sure, but lest every song you write have seven brilliant stanzas, each with a pre-chorus, with each verse covering everything from nuclear war to poverty to Paul's doctrine of atonement to Vatican II to what you had for breakfast, you *must* find a way to boil it down.

Sometimes I make maple syrup. There's a grandfather of a maple tree in the woods near our house, and one day I googled "How to make maple syrup." As it turns out, it's not that hard if you have an afternoon on your hands. I ordered the spile, which is the little metal tap you hammer into a predrilled hole in the trunk. As soon as that thing is in the tree, sap starts dripping. It's amazing. You hook a bucket to the spile and come back the next day to a sloshing, watery bucketful of sap. But maple sap isn't what you think. It's water, basically. There's not much sugar in there, so you literally have to boil it down. A lot. You get one gallon of maple syrup for every forty gallons of sap, which is why real maple syrup costs a fortune. It took hours of stirring, watching the sap level in the big pot, adding sap, stirring, watching it boil down, squinting through the sweet-smelling steam, until the magic moment when the bubbles get really small and threaten to boil over. Then you remove it from the heat and call your wife and kids and neighbors in to look at the magic syrup you got by hammering some metal into a tree.

Then, of course, you make pancakes.

If you were to taste the maple sap before you boiled it down, which I did, you'd find it hard to believe there's any sweetness hiding in there at all. Now imagine dumping a sloshy bucket of that watery sap on a plate of pancakes. Trust me, the kids wouldn't eat it. That's what it's like to listen to a song that's about everything instead of one thing—it ends up being about nothing at all. Whether you're writing a sermon, a poem, or a mystery novel, you have to do the work of boiling it down. But it's important to remember that you don't *start* with the syrup. You start with the sap, and then you get selective. That's what you have to do with all your big ideas. Find out what's essential, what's sweetest, and boil away the rest. One great example is a song by a band called Fountains of Wayne. It's called "All Kinds of Time," and is a brilliant example of selectivity. Once again, put down this book, head over to your computer, and give the song a listen.

See what I mean? It's a one-inch picture frame if I ever saw one. The song is zoomed in on what's happening inside of one person in a matter of seconds—five, maybe ten—and it takes four minutes to tell about it. In that one glimpse, you get into the quarterback's head and heart, you learn about his wild dreams, about his family and his fiancé, you're reminded of that wondrous, storybook thing that can happen in sports, a thing that no one can really explain but which commentators talk about for days, when the stars align and against all hope someone does something amazing, something they'll probably never do again but which feels like fate and somehow they know it's going to work before they do it, and then the crowd is on its feet and the good guys win and for a few minutes all is right with the world. The fact that it seems to be happening at a high school football game makes it even more poignant because we all know that the quarterback's life is about to get much, much more complicated, and he'll probably always look back at that moment and wonder what happened to all that time that once seemed so abundant.

Selectivity means choosing what *not* to say. It means aiming at the bull's-eye. It means making sure the song is about one specific thing so that when folks are driving home from the show, they can say, "Remember the one he wrote for his son?"

The Gospels make up a very small portion of Scripture. And they only tell about a small portion of Jesus' time on earth. At the end of John's Gospel he talks about selectivity: "Now there are also many other things that Jesus did. Were every one of them to be written, I suppose that the world itself could not contain the books that would be written" (John 21:25). By the guidance of the Holy Spirit, certain things were left out of the story and certain things, the things we needed, were selected to remain. To carry the principle one step further, the Incarnation itself is a remarkable example of what I'm talking about. God, full of all power and glory, utterly unapproachable by mortals, became flesh and dwelt among us. The incomprehensible, uncontainable God became a man with whom we could walk, talk, and eat. He spoke through his creation, but we didn't listen. He had spoken through the prophets, but we didn't listen. Then he became a man with a mouth, spoke to his disciples, demonstrated the nature of the Father's love, and though it's true that some still didn't listen, some did, and the world has never been the same. Jesus, a concentration of all the thunder of God's glory, looked us in the eye and opened his glorious heart to his sons and daughters.

The gospel is the sweetest thing I know.

12

DISCIPLINE

I f only you would apply yourself."

My teachers in high school told me that so often that they decided to really drill it in by writing it in my yearbook, over and over. I was a bad student. Still am. Busywork was the bane of my existence—those little homework assignments that felt like a waste of time, that required organizational skills like Writing Down Your Assignment and Not Losing Your Handout. These were difficult tasks for me. My locker was a pile of loose papers that got more and more crinkly as the weeks went on until it looked like the inside of a recycling bin. I discovered that if you ignore something long enough, it really does go away. Literally. The papers would disintegrate. I would pass just enough tests and do enough begging to eke by with a D. Sometimes.

I failed Geometry and Spanish, and had to take summer school. Some people thrive with structure, or so I hear. They like being given a list of tasks and get some sick thrill out of actually completing them. It's crazy, I tell you. I'm not wired that way. I get an actual physical sensation of dread and anxiety and panic whenever I'm told to do something menial. You can ask Jamie. Bless her heart, she's had to learn a lot of patience over the years, because when there's a pesky home repair issue she knows I'll put it off as long as possible. If it even *sort of* works, it doesn't get fixed until I'm in the exact right mood to do it, which can take months.

More often than not I'll wait until the thing is too broken to ignore, and then when it only takes five minutes I wonder why on earth I didn't do it two months ago. The same is true with mailing stuff. I'll write a letter or thank-you note, seal it, and then realize I don't have a stamp. That thing will sit there for months before I muster the energy to actually go to the post office. It's pathetic, really, but whatever psychological flaw causes this behavior has been there since I was little and has caused me no end of trouble.

And yet, and yet, there's another behavior, an obsessive one that has served me well. While my teachers were writing notes to my parents about my bad grades, I was sitting at the church piano practicing for hours on end, making up songs, learning others. I was filling sketchpads with drawings, journaling consistently, listening to music, and absorbing books.

When we moved to The Warren, the woods were a claustrophobic tangle of thorn, privet, and bush honeysuckle. (Don't be fooled by the name—bush honeysuckle is hellish.) Jamie and the kids and I crouched our way under the brushy eaves, lopping branches here and there, looking for good trees, marveling at huge slabs of limestone and granite peeking out of the soil, wondering how all those old brown beer bottles ended up under the humus so far from the house. Eventually, we cut a series of trails guided by the shape of the land and the fattest trees we could find, mostly cedar and hackberry, but along the way we discovered a couple of young sugar maples, a beast of a Shumard oak, and the Goliath of our woods—a massive tree that neither of the two experts I've brought out here could identify. "It looks like a white walnut," one of them said, "but if it is, that's the biggest one in Tennessee."

At the center of our little woods is the bowl of what used to be a cattle pond, now a marshy wetland thick with waist-high grass and a few willows. When we get a lot of rain there's a trickle that runs through the center and disappears into the foot of the old earthen dam someone piled up a generation or two ago. The former owner, who grew up here, said that he remembered ice-skating on the pond as a boy. The pond (the non-pond, rather) is a feature of our property I can't stop thinking about. From our first day here seven years ago, I've voiced my desire to repair the dam and clear out the brush so that we can have a little fishing hole, something not just for the grandchildren but as a food source in case there's an invasion like the one in *Red Dawn*. I'm only half-kidding. Something about having a few acres wakes up the survivalist in a man, which is part of why I so enjoy gardening nowadays. The less I depend on the machine the more connected I feel to the remnants of Eden shimmering at the edges of the natural world. Before you think me too hippie, I should remind you that I'm writing this on a computer, and I enjoy my Netflix account.

I'm not sure why I'm telling you all this, except to say that I've always had a thing for big projects—not busywork. For example, the boys and I chainsawed and hacked and lopped the swath of trees between our house and the pond a few years ago, clearing a section of the slope about twenty yards wide and thirty yards deep—an enormous amount of work that rewarded us with a clear view of the non-pond from the kitchen window. The morning after the clearing was complete I looked down the hill to discover a family of deer drinking from the trickle. Of course, I thought, they've probably been drinking down there all these years but we never knew it till now. The fact that the trees are gone hasn't frightened them off, either, so almost every day I see those beauties graze their way through the bowl.

Here's a strange memory: when I was a kid in Illinois I discovered a pile of shoveled sidewalk snow in someone's front yard. At some point I decided that that snowpile needed a boy-sized tunnel dug right through the center, so on the way home from kindergarten I stopped every day for about a week and worked, though I had no idea whose house it was. After fifteen minutes or so I'd head home so my mom wouldn't be worried. All day at school my mind was occupied with that tunnel. It wasn't as if I had never dug a tunnel in the snow before, and I've often wondered why I remember this one so vividly. But there was something simple and delightful to my little six-year-old self about working at this tunnel alone, in secret, a little at a time for a whole week. The day I finally broke through to the other side I brushed the snow off my pants and stood there, mittened hands on my hips, admiring my work. Then I felt someone watching me. I turned around and saw a woman in the house at the window, peeking out at me with a kind face. She might have waved. I pretended not to see her. I was deeply embarrassed as I realized that she had probably been watching me for days.

Memories choose us. Of all the things that must have happened during my childhood—little adventures, moments of shame or joy or comfort—only a few images, like this one, rise to the surface. And they don't just rise once. They come to me again and again as if there's some mystery hidden in all the plainness, as if someday I'll wake up in the middle of the night and understand why that snow tunnel is stuck in my head.

The next week as I passed the house (on the other side of the street) I noticed that the pile was gone. I've always suspected that the woman and her husband never intended to leave it by their driveway, but they noticed a little boy stopping to dig every day and graced me with a week of peaceful, pointless work. I wonder if it gave her something to do, someone to watch for, something to talk about with her husband at dinner during a long, featureless winter.

Earlier today I was working on a new song, alone in the house, and it felt just like digging. I wonder if someone was watching from a high window?

While the obsessive tendency can be a boon to someone with a career in the arts, the thing can come back to bite you. Because, like it or not, if you want to get paid to do this stuff you have to actually do the work. And once you realize you're responsible for your family by either caring for the children or providing a full-time income, art—no matter how fun it was in the beginning—becomes work. It becomes a chore. It becomes burdensome. It's suddenly so much easier to get excited about that *other* project that just won't leave you alone. And so you start something new, which is natural and quite welcome. But then that gets old and you start four more new things, and you realize you've bitten off more than you can chew and nothing gets done, least of all the project that got you going in the first place. So as much as I may gripe about my teachers and parents and the busywork I was expected to do, there comes a time for us all when we have to reckon with it. Sometimes you have to do the work even if you don't feel like it. Sometimes you have to put away your wants and do what needs to be done, which really means dying to self in order to find life. This is a way of practicing resurrection.

In the last chapter of Roald Dahl's Boy: *Tales of Childhood*, he says that he worked for a few years as a businessman.

> I enjoyed it, I really did. I began to realize how simple life could be if one had a regular routine to follow with fixed hours and a fixed salary and very little original thinking to do. The life of a writer is absolute hell compared with the life of a businessman. The writer has to force himself to work. He has to make his own hours and if he doesn't go to his desk at all there is nobody to scold him. If he is a writer of fiction he lives in a world of fear. Each new day demands new ideas and he can never be sure whether he is going to come up with them or not. Two hours of writing fiction leaves this particular writer absolutely drained. For those two hours he has been miles away, he has been somewhere else, in a different place with totally different people, and the effort of swimming back into normal surroundings is very great. It is almost a

shock. The writer walks out of his workroom in a daze. He wants a drink. He needs it. It happens to be a fact that nearly every writer of fiction in the world drinks more whisky than is good for him. He does it to give himself faith, hope and courage. A person is a fool to become a writer.[8]

I wasn't expecting to read a paragraph that encouraging when I started that book. I suspect a businessman would read that paragraph and wonder what all the fuss is about. It might sound an awful lot like complaining. But it isn't. I sighed a weary, happy sigh because Dahl assured me I'm not as crazy or as wimpy as I'm afraid I am. The same can be said for song-writing too. God has arranged the process (for me, at least) in such a way that after every song is complete, I get amnesia. I think, in the fast-fading thrill of having written a song, that I've finally unlocked the secret formula, discovered the missing number, solved the timeless mystery of how to write a song. I have at last answered for myself the question of whether the music or the lyrics come first! And the answer is—wait, I had it a second ago. What was it again? And it's gone. Even as the last note fades to silence, amnesia sets in. I can't remember how it works. So the next time I pick up the guitar or open the notebook, I do so with fear and trembling, unsure how to proceed. I'm starting from zero.

It's a wonder anything ever gets written.

---

8. Roald Dahl, *Boy: Tales of Childhood* (New York: Puffin Books, 1999).

It made me wonder, why did he write at all? Dahl confesses a disbelief in God based mostly on his abuse at the hands of several wicked men of the Church—and it's hard to blame him. It's struggle enough to believe, even without a priest beating you with a cane. Then why did he suffer the long toil of the written word? Where did that urge come from? That he wrote books for children makes me think that the suffering of his own youth softened his heart toward the young. Perhaps he hoped to give them some light, some escape, some comfort in their own fear. He was beaten by wretched men at boarding schools, made to bleed, made to grab his ankles and weep while they hit him, sometimes while the Headmaster quoted Scripture. It's fascinating that this poor boy grew into a tough man who would work to spin fantastical stories for children.

But in this book especially, his descriptions of people, and of the beauties and horrors of his childhood, were vivid. Dahl remembered what it was like to be a little boy. And he remembered that it is terrifying. It reminded me how vital it is that Christians bend low and speak tenderly to the children in our lives. These boys and girls at our churches, in our schools, down the street, are living a harrowing adventure. Every one of them falls into one of two categories: wounded, or soon-to-be-wounded. The depth and nature of those wounds will vary, but they're all malleable souls in a world clanging with hammer blows. The bigger they get, the easier the target. I get a lump in my throat every night I sing "After the Last Tear Falls" (which I cowrote with Andrew Osenga), when I get to the line: "After the last young girl's innocence is stolen . . . there is love." It's because I'm certain there are people in the audience for whom that line must trigger a terrible memory. I sing the final chorus with all the ache I can muster because I want them to believe that love outlives all the pain that ever was.

Those of us who write, who sing, who paint, must remember that to a child a song may glow like a nightlight in a scary bedroom. It may be the only thing holding back the monsters. That story may be the only beautiful, true thing that makes it through all the ugliness of a little girl's world to rest in her secret heart. May we take that seriously. It is our job, it is our ministry, it is the sword we swing in the Kingdom, to remind children that the good guys win, that the stories are true, and that a fool's hope may be the best kind.

If you're called to do this sort of work, then keep those dear ones in your mind as you fight your way up the long mountain of obedience. You'll be tempted to slow down, or take an easier route—but it is only by discipline that you'll finish, and it is only in finishing that you'll be able to offer up your humble work to those weary souls who may need it.

Remember my high school buddy, Wade the Conundrum, with the makeshift studio in the single-wide? For years I had tried to record stuff at home using whatever was lying around, so when I heard about the Tascam four-track, it was the only thing I could think about. I had to have one. Just imagine the breezy openness of not just one or two tracks, and not even a paltry three, but *four*. Such options! I could do anything.

I imagined my creative production would quadruple in proportion with the possible track count. But after goofing around with it for a few months and achieving less-than-mediocre results, I was left with the stark reality that four tracks wouldn't make me any better at songwriting. Not really. Now, if I had sixteen tracks, with compression and reverb and a decent mic and an isolation booth, *then* I could make something awesome. But until then it was just a guitar and a notebook. *Someday*, I thought. Someday there would be nothing to hold me back.

Fast-forward to the ubiquity of Apple Computers. An app called GarageBand is about as accessible as it gets, and according to a quick search online just now, it maxes out at around 255 tracks, which is pretty ridiculous. I was so excited to utilize GarageBand for the writing process, and to be honest, it's pretty wonderful for my meager needs. But after that initial flash of "All right, *now* I can finally realize my potential," the magic fades and you realize that you're still stuck with, well, you.

A few years ago I had to give up the space I rented in the loft of my neighbor's old log cabin. For about two years I had nowhere to go to work on songs in private, which meant working in the corner of the living room or squatting at someone's studio or, if the weather was nice, sitting on the bench at the bend in the trail until the mosquitoes became unbearable. When we moved to The Warren, my dream was to one day build the perfect little writer's cabin, an idyllic retreat where I'd write book after book and song after song while observing the slow opening of gladioli in the garden. Thanks to some very kind people who helped me out, I was able to build a dream studio called The Chapter House. It's hard to say who's happier—Jamie or me. I'm glad to have a peaceful space to work, and a place for my book collection and my guitars; she's glad that all those books and guitar cases aren't piled up in the corner of our bedroom anymore.

The first few weeks I would literally thank God out loud when I walked in here. I'd look out the window at the swaying maples and grin like an idiot because God had blessed me with exactly the kind of space I hoped against hope for.

And then.

Then, I sat down to write—and slammed into that familiar, foreboding wall that some people call writer's block. It was the same thing I had encountered first with the four-track, then with GarageBand. It doesn't matter how many gadgets you have, or how much time and space you have, or how good your guitar is. At the end of the day, it's just you and the song; you and the story. Don't get me wrong, it's a huge blessing to have a space, or a computer, or a nice-sounding guitar. But Ivan Drago had all the best training equipment in the world, and Rocky still clobbered him. You can't blame your equipment. You can't blame your lack of time. You can't blame your upbringing. Either you're willing to steward the gift God gave you by stepping into the ring and fighting for it, or you spend your life in training, cashing in excuse after excuse until there's no time left, no fight left, no song, no story.

In terms of money, it doesn't really cost anything to write. (It's quite expensive in other ways.) Publishing is another matter, but the actual writing requires nothing but a pen and paper, and the self-discipline to write. Tolkien started The Hobbit on the back of some papers he was grading. On any trip to the Hard Rock Cafe you'll see hotel napkins and scraps of paper on which some of the world's greatest songs were written. The secret is that there is no secret. All you need is to force your-self to do it. And I happen to think that our distraction-laced culture, at least in the West, makes what used to be a matter of course into a matter of extreme measures. I don't think anyone would disagree that we have far more distractions than they did one hundred years ago—heck, *ten* years ago.

Once I heard Anne Lamott speak to a group of writers, and she said, "The best thing you can do to write your book is to stop *not* doing it. Just stop it." Stop making excuses, she said, and pointed out that she wrote her first few books as a single mom with a screaming baby, not to mention a drug habit.

When I started the book you're reading, I was in the studio setting sail in a tiny boat, with Gabe Scott as my captain, trying to cross the sea of another album. When we finally debarked on the far shore it was a country called *The Burning Edge of Dawn*. That was years ago. I've been working on this manuscript off and on since then, and it's ironic that the cycle has come back around and I'm back at it, writing for a new album. It's an album called *Resurrection Letters, Volume I*, the prequel to *Volume II*, which came out about ten years ago. If you're reading this and thinking, "Wow, what a cool idea," let me stop you right there. It was a terrible idea. This album about the Resurrection of Jesus has been haunting me for years, mainly because the subject matter is of the utmost importance, and I don't feel equal to the task. Not only that, people who liked volume *two* have been asking me about this one all this time, and will have high (perhaps unreasonable) expectations. My hope is that, after I finish this book, I'll get my guitar out of the case, lean it against the wall by the piano, then get on my knees and pray that fine old Bach prayer, "Jesu juva." I want to be obedient to my calling, but I'm afraid. He's given me songs before, frail though they may be. Why should this be so hard? After all, I believe in the Resurrection—that of Jesus and of those who belong to him; Ben Shive, who's producing this album, is possibly the most talented person I know, and knows Scripture far better than I do; the label is helping me pay for it; I have friends who are much better songwriters than I am, a phone call away for either advice or collaboration. I have everything I need.

Everything but the songs.

A confession: I don't think I can do it.

I've done the very best I can do already, and I'm afraid that God will remove the Spirit from me, that whatever that thing is that makes the songs work, the mystical gas in the engine, will be cut off, this thing will slow to a trickle and die, and I'll put out an album that people hate. They'll say to each other in hushed tones that something was just missing, that the songs were hokey, that they weren't clever enough, that the melodies were ho-hum, that I was repeating myself, that I was trying too hard, that I cheesed out, that my voice was just too nasally, that the chord progressions were overused, that it sounded too much like my other stuff and I wasn't taking risks, that I was taking too many risks and it sounded like I was trying to prove something or to be pathetically hip. Or maybe God will finally have had enough of my sin, my pride, my lust, my resentment, my self-centeredness, and if I haven't learned my lesson by now then he's going to have to take drastic measures and really serve me up some failure on a grand scale.

I've sat at the piano for hours already, looking for lyrics and melodies, but everything sounds the same and I feel as uninspired as ever. Does it mean I'm finished? A more sobering thought: if I'm finished, would I miss it? But the truth is, I've been here before. Many times. We all have. So how do we find the faith to press on?

Remember. Remember, Hebrew children, who you once were in Egypt. Remember the altars set up along the way to remind yourselves that you made the journey and God rescued you from sword and famine, from chariots and pestilence, that once you were there, but now you are here. It *happened.* Our memories are fallible, residing in that most complex and mysterious organ in the human body (and therefore the known universe), capable of being suppressed, manipulated, altered, but also profoundly powerful and able to transport a person to a place fifty years ago all because of a whiff of your grandfather's cologne or an old book or the salty air. *As often as you do this, do it in remembrance of me. Remember with every sip of wine that we shared this meal, you and I.* Remember.

So I look at the last album, the last book, and am forced to admit that I didn't know anymore then than I do now. Every song is an Ebenezer stone, evidence of God's faithfulness. I just need to remember. Trust is crucial. So is self-forgetfulness and risk and a measure of audacity. And now that I think about it, there's also wonder, insight, familiarity with Scripture, passion, a good night's sleep, breakfast (preferably an egg sandwich), an encouraging voice, diligence, patience. I need silence. Privacy. Time—that's what I need: more time. But first I need a vacation, because I've been really grinding away at this other stuff and my mental cache is full. A deadline would be great. I work best with deadlines, and maybe some bills piling up. Some new guitar strings would help, and a nice candle. And that's *all* I need, in the words of Steve Martin's *The Jerk*.

This is the truth: all I really need is a guitar, some paper, and discipline. If only I would apply myself.

———

A few years ago, after the kids went to bed I climbed the cold hill in the dark from The Warren to what used to be my office, determined to write chapter 32 of my new book before I went to sleep. I don't know why, but that chapter was exceedingly hard to get my head around.

At about 1:00 a.m. I pinned it down. Or maybe I set it free. I could hardly hold my eyes open, but I managed to perform my chapter-finishing ritual: (a) save the document called "Chapter 32"; (b) copy and paste it into the body of the document called "All Chapters" so I can see my word count and page number; and (c) feel like I've accomplished something. It's a good feeling, and on nights like that night, a hard-earned one. It's the same feeling I get when I finish a five-mile run, or when I cut off the lawn mower, or when I lean my guitar case in the corner of the family room after a long weekend of shows. Good work means good rest.

This is what I wrote in my journal that night:

> *The walk down the hill to our sleepy house was the crossing of a threshold. It was a transition from the*

world of "what if?" to the world of "what is." The grass under my boots is something I don't have to work to describe in a story—God did the work already, and I just have to walk. He described it and so it is. What a thing it is to walk on the grass of God's imagination. The glow I see in the window is from an actual lamp on an actual nightstand, where I know a book is waiting to be read. I hear my dog in the woods. I remember that his echoing baritone bark is made up of actual sound waves crashing out of his throat to ricochet off the trunks of the juniper, honey locust, and hackberry trees where an actual opossum is trembling in the brush. I sense these things on the cold walk home, and I marvel at this world God thought up. In the words of poet Richard Wilbur, "The world is fundamentally a great wonder."

I am convinced that poets are toddlers in a cathedral, slobbering on wooden blocks and piling them up in the light of the stained glass. We can hardly make anything beautiful that wasn't beautiful in the first place. We aren't writers so much as gleeful rearrangers of words whose meanings we can't begin to know. When we manage to make something pretty, it's only so because we are ourselves a flourish on a greater canvas. That means there's no end to the discovery. We may crawl around the cathedral floor for ages before we grow up enough to reach the doorknob and walk outside into a garden of delights. Beyond that, the city, then the rolling hills, then the sea. And when the world of every cell has been limned and painted and sung, we lie back on the grass, satisfied that our work is done. Then, of course, the sun sets and we see above us the dark dome of glittering stars.

On and on it goes, all the way to the lightless borderlands of time and space, which we come to discover in some future age are but the beginnings or endings of a single word spoken from the mouth of God. Some nights, while I traipse down the hill, I imagine that word isn't a word at all, but a burst of laughter.

13

DISCERNMENT

When my daughter was about five she was already writing songs. I decided early on that I would rather my children listen to a great song by someone who wasn't a Christian than a bad song by someone who was, so my kids grew up on not just Switchfoot and Rich Mullins but also Paul Simon and Counting Crows and James Taylor. I also wanted to teach them that good music transcends genre, so we listened to plenty of bluegrass, folk, pop, rock and roll, movie soundtracks, and hymns.

"This," I told my daughter when she was tiny, "is a song by a woman named Alison Krauss and her band, Union Station. Her voice is one of the finest on the planet." Skye listened to Alison constantly. One of the first songs we ever sang together was called "Country Boy," and Alison's recording remains one of the saddest and prettiest things I know.

Some well-meaning soul gave Skye a CD one day and I recoiled with horror when I saw the hot-pink cover. It was a CD of "tween" praise and worship songs and the cover featured four well-meaning teenybopper girls with flying-V electric guitars. There might have been some lightning bolts and smiley butterflies thrown in for good measure. Repulsed by the thought that she would fall in love with it and we'd have to endure Bad Music for the foreseeable future, I planned to sneak the CD away before Skye had a chance to listen to it. But, as if in slow motion, she grabbed the CD and tore off the cellophane, then jammed it into the minivan's player. It was like the slow-motion end of *The Untouchables* or something, only I wasn't able to stop her in time. Sure enough, the music was terrible, and I drove sulkily, hands at ten and two, trying to figure out a way to repair the damage. Before twenty seconds had passed, little eight-year-old Skye ejected the CD with a wince of distaste and said, "I don't like it. Can we just listen to Alison Krauss instead?"

That, dear reader, was one of my greatest parenting victories.

There's a balance, to be sure, but I actually want my children to have a bit of healthy snobbery about the art they consume. Jamie wants our kids to eat good food, and part of that means helping them develop a taste for kale and Brussels sprouts and fruit.. The goal is to get them to recognize that some foods are good for you and some are bad, and not just to make the right choices but to realize that your body actually *wants* you to make the right choice. You feel terrible after McDonald's. You feel great after sushi. For your body's sake, you might have to learn to like sushi.

Art is the same. I've taken it upon myself to teach the kids the artistic equivalent of junk food—stuff that's an easy sell, made for money, banal at best, and corrupt at worst—so they would know that while it's okay to have a few guilty pleasures, it's better to seek out that which edifies, enlightens, strengthens, and to do so more and more over time. If you want to be an artist, you have to cultivate artistic discernment.

We're swimming in a tidal wave of entertainment in the form of music and television and film and billboards and magazines—a deluge like the world has never known. A thousand years ago no one would dream that the story they wrote might be turned into moving pictures that were viewed multiple times by millions and millions of people—but here we are. Not only that, the art is driven by the machine of capitalism and commerce, which means the artist has to try that much harder to maintain any aesthetic integrity in order to make something beautiful while straining to meet the industry's understandable need for a return on investment. The problem, according to G. K. Chesterton, is that all democracies eventually vote themselves out of existence. Long-term, the majority won't choose what's best for it. The masses—or at least those who don't aspire to any sense of discernment—tend to choose the path of least resistance, which means the most bankable art is often the most vapid and loveless: noise, noise, noise. A clanging cymbal.

The better path, the path of discernment, is the steeper trail with the heart-stopping view. Discernment demands more from a film or a song than mere entertainment, asks questions about content and intent. Discernment means reading the nutritional facts on the back of the box, asking what the ingredients are, and if there's a bunch of high-fructose corn syrup and monosodium glutamate, for goodness sake *choose something else*. I'm not saying you can't watch the fifteenth *Pirates of the Caribbean* film, just don't go and sit there like a bump on a log, drinking it all down, without asking yourself if it's actually any good, let alone good for you. When the film is over, think about what was really going on, about the subtext (if there is any), about the themes, if there's anything there that's true, or excellent, or worthy of praise. I can hear you saying, "But sometimes I just want to turn off my brain and watch something fun." To that I say, "Fine. But there are really *good* fun movies, too. Wouldn't it be better to give your ten bucks to the people working overtime to entertain while also striving for something truly artful? (Some of the Pixar films come to mind.)

Paul Simon's *Graceland* is one of the finest albums ever made, and was a staple in our minivan when the kids were young. There are so many fun, entertaining sounds and grooves, but it's also *about* something—whether it's commentary on war or a longing for grace or the futility of technological progress. You can make a record that is unapologetically rock and roll just because rock and roll can be a blast (thinking now of the first Raconteurs album, or some of the Colony House or Leagues stuff), but it's so well done that it's more like a delicious homemade cookie at grandma's house than a store-bought box of generic Chips Ahoy. If you want to eat the processed stuff once in a while, fine. Just realize that there's something better out there.

Disclaimer: there's a danger in getting carried away. The kind of "healthy snobbery" I'm talking about can quickly turn into a highfalutin elitism, which is unhealthy and even destructive. More times than I care to admit, I've expressed a strong opinion on a work of art and realized too late that I was bullying others into seeing things my way. The key is to delight in what you find delightful more than you bemoan what isn't. Nobody likes feeling belittled.

Aesthetic discernment also drives you to work that much harder when you're making your own art. If you know that

Springsteen's "Thunder Road" is a great song—a proper Great Song, mind you—then you hold your own song about youth and redemption up to it and ask yourself, "Am I even close to that kind of awesomeness?" (The answer will be "no.") Then you keep working, keep straining toward a level of excellence that will most likely elude you forever, but it's the only way your songs are ever going to move from bad to decent to good. You will probably never write a song as good as Rich Mullins's best stuff (I know I won't), but you have to try. And you have to keep trying.

Become a student of the craft. Have conversations with people whose insight dwarfs your own; they'll teach you what to look for. Not long after moving to Nashville I realized that I didn't like Bob Dylan. But no self-respecting songwriter could ignore the entire catalog of one of the most celebrated songwriters in history, so I decided to eat my vegetables. I asked Randall Goodgame, a Dylan fan, which album to start with, and he told me, "*Blood on the Tracks*, no question." I bought it and listened. It wasn't easy. But after about the tenth spin, that gravelly voice was no longer grating and the genius of the poetry became more and more apparent, and just like that I became a fan. It would be hard to pinpoint any demonstrable influence of Dylan's writing on my own, but I have no doubt that I have been enriched by Dylan's lyrics and learned from him a lot more about what makes for a good song.

It was the same with poetry. Other than Silverstein's *Where the Sidewalk Ends* I was skeptical of modern poetry and mostly ignorant of older stuff. Then at a retreat my friend Al Andrews recited a Billy Collins poem called "The Revenant." (Once again, you should probably google it and read it right now.) I was staggered, not only by the poem itself but by its effect on the room. The next day Al read something by Mary Oliver, and I began to think that perhaps there was something to this whole "poetry" thing. First I read Collins's *Sailing Alone Around the Room*, then *Nine Horses*, then I fell into Wendell Berry's Sabbath poems, and then more Mary Oliver, then Heaney, Hopkins, Shaw, Levertov, and so on. I'm not saying I'm some kind of expert on poetry, but after having read it for a few years I at least know something of what it's capable of, and now when I write my own poems it's humbling to realize how difficult it is to produce something effective, let alone beautiful—whether or not it rhymes.

A few years ago a woman approached me after a concert. She explained that we had met about ten years earlier, and she had asked me to write some songwriting advice along with my signature on one of my old records. "Oh, no," I said with a grimace, remembering how much worse my know-it-all tendencies used to be. "What did I write?" She smiled and opened the CD case. There it was in my handwriting, written with a Sharpie:

> *Don't write bad songs.*
> —*Andrew Peterson*

I blushed. "I'm sorry. What an arrogant thing to say."

"No, it's okay," she said. "You explained what you meant— that I should try hard not to settle." She was being very gracious, because I know I probably felt really cool and edgy writing it at the time. She told me Andy Gullahorn had been at the same show, standing across the church lobby from me. She had taken the CD over to him and asked him to write some songwriting advice, too. "He saw what you wrote," she said, "and then added this." She turned the CD booklet over and showed me Gully's signature. Next to his name he had written, "Write the bad ones, too."

Touché, Gullahorn. I see what you did there.

He's exactly right. And in a sense, so am I. While it's important to cultivate discernment, to work as hard as possible to do excellent work, to try really hard to make your song *not* bad, it's just as important—perhaps more so, in the beginning—to make *something*, even if it's not great. Don't let your inner critic keep you from writing. Know that your songs aren't going to be perfect. Then as joyfully as possible, keep writing. The only way to get better at something is to practice. It's like we all have a quota of bad songs we have to meet before we get to a good one, so it's best to start chipping away at the quota now. The sooner you start, the sooner you'll learn. Besides, a "bad" song lovingly written for a friend, family member, or neighbor will be a far greater blessing to them than a great song you never wrote at all. In that sense, the world needs more bad songs.

I wrote a poem after a conversation with the great Jimmy Abegg a few years ago. If you don't know Jimmy A, you've probably heard his genius guitar work on some Rich Mullins records. He's all over A *Liturgy, a Legacy, and a Ragamuffin Band*. He's also a successful painter, with work hanging in galleries around the country. We were having lunch at Baja Burrito, talking about success, failure, and creativity, and that led to this:

What Jimmy A Taught Me about Art

As long as you're making *something*,
Jimmy told me,

Then failure is a word
That has no meaning.

And so, I wrote this poem.

There's a tension, to be sure, between holding yourself to a progressively higher bar while staying brave enough to put pen to paper. But if you maintain the posture of a student eager to learn the craft, you'll gradually improve without realizing it. *After* you've made something, go back in a few weeks and critique it with a gentle heart. As difficult as it is, go back and listen to recordings of your concerts. Identify the things that aren't working. Then go do another show. Don't write bad songs—but write the bad ones, too.

When it comes to discernment and serving the audience, there's another tension at work. What's the balance between giving the audience what they want and giving them what (you think) they need? The *Behold the Lamb of God* Christmas tour has always featured a songwriter-in-the-round format for the first half of the show. It's likely that most of the crowd isn't used to acoustic storytime shows, so they show up expecting more of a pageant. Over the years I got the occasional complaint that the first half of the show was too acoustic, too long, and most of the songs were from singer-songwriters they'd never heard of. I'm a people pleaser, so that bugged me. Then I looked at my friends on the stage, playing their guitars and singing their hearts out; I also saw certain people in the audience locked in to those songs like a space freighter to a tractor beam. So I decided not to worry about it. Yes, I hope the whole audience loves every minute of the concert, but I also happen to think that it's okay if not all of these songs are for the whole audience. Maybe this one song is for that one person on the second row. Like it or not, folks, we'll be serving some veggies with the meal. Maybe if you hear enough Dylan you'll realize how good he is. Don't worry, though. We're here to serve, so there's plenty of dessert to go around.

My neighbor was dying. Bob and Darlene had been married for fifty-some years, and he wanted to surprise her with a song called "Love Me, But Let Me Go." He wrote the verses on his deathbed and asked if I'd put them to music. Bob wasn't a professional songwriter. He was a husband and a father. Do you think I spent one second being critical of his poetic form, his use of metaphor, his sense of rhythm? None of that mattered. It was a great honor to add a melody and record it for his sweet wife to listen to after he was gone. Bob wrote an honest expression of love to his wife, and that was more than enough. It ought to be a matter of course in our culture that members of every household show love to each other through poems, letters, or pictures, and do so fearlessly, without intimidation, without a thought about marketability.

I want to reiterate that the principle of discernment is not about lording artistic eliteness over people. That would only serve to sequester art into the realm of the expert, shutting down our God-given impulse to love with what we make. Cultivating discernment is a good thing for everyone, but I'm speaking here to those of us who are called to the long road of learning a craft. In that sense, we're called to write not only for our immediate community but for those who come after us. I feel an obligation to love them too. For your work to survive that long, either you have to be a genius or you have to submit yourself to a lifelong apprenticeship, clinging to a willingness to learn from the masters.

I'm not interested in making a name for myself (not on my good days, anyway). But when I read a four-hundred-year-old George Herbert poem and tears spring to my eyes at the wideness of God's love, I'm grateful that he was a student of the craft. Otherwise, his work wouldn't have made its way to my bookshelf in The Chapter House. Imagine traveling back in time to seventeenth-century Cambridge and telling George Herbert to keep working, keep writing, keep learning his craft, because his poem "Love (III)," about Jesus' great mercy, would one day make a room full of bearded Nashville dudes cry. (True story. It happened just a few weeks ago.)

Maybe the song you're writing is for one specific heartbroken soul who won't be born for another four hundred years. Maybe you won't meet him or her until the New Creation, and they'll thank you for opening yourself to public scrutiny, for striving to arrange the words just so, for learning about what makes for a good melody or tight phrasing.

By God's grace, those little differences may be the bursts of wind that carry the song across the sea of time.

14

ART NOURISHES COMMUNITY

Most people know that C. S. Lewis and J. R. R. Tolkien were friends, and that their friendship was part of what led Lewis to Christ. But a lesser-known part of their story is that Lewis is largely responsible for *The Lord of the Rings*.

Whenever the Inklings got together to drink and smoke and laugh, they often shared whatever they were writing at the time, and some of the members of their little society weren't too crazy about Tolkien's sprawling epic. Tolkien wasn't sure anyone would care about his nerdy fantasy world or his elvish language, and over the twelve years it took him to write what would later be known as one of the century's greatest works of literature, he despaired of ever finishing it. Anyone who's tried to write much of anything at all has had the same terrible feeling—that all your work is a waste of time, that no one could possibly care about it, that there are better things to do. But Lewis *loved* "the new hobbit," as they called it, and pestered Tolkien again and again to finish the book. Diana Pavlac Glyer, in her wonderful book *Bandersnatch*, chronicles this remarkable friendship and identifies several aspects of it that contributed to the flourishing of their craft. She says that artists need "resonators." They need someone who gets what you're trying to do, who is moved by your work and will encourage you to keep fighting when the battle is long. Lewis was Tolkien's resonator, and now, all these years later, we get to read about Frodo and Sam. Thank God for resonators.

When I was in Bible College I was playing at a junior high lock-in. If you don't know what a lock-in is, then be grateful. It's an all-nighter for a church youth group and is one of the things that is wrong with the world. There's way too much Mountain Dew, way too many dark closets for two people to smooch in during hide-and-seek, way too many tears shed around 5:00 a.m. when everybody's emotional but they don't know why. And then, of course, the parents have to deal with their kids' dazed and confused looks for the next few days.

A youth-pastor buddy of mine asked if I would come and sing at the 2:00 a.m. slot, and I told him no. I had other, less harrowing things to do that night. But then he offered me $60 and I agreed without hesitation. One of the poor chaperones happened to be a college student named Gabe Scott, and I heard from someone that he played guitar. After my pathetic set, we ducked into the pastor's office and played music until sunrise. He was a Randy Stonehill guy, I was a Rich Mullins guy, and we kept trying to one-up the other guy's cover, finally finding some common ground in the Steven Curtis Chapman/ Geoff Moore duet "Listen to Our Hearts," which we played flaw- lessly the first time, each of us happening to have learned the complementing parts on our own. That was in 1995 and we're still friends. In fact, he produced *The Burning Edge of Dawn* in 2015. There are two morals to this story: (1) Say yes to every gig in the beginning, because you never know what might happen. (2) It turns out Randy Stonehill has some pretty great songs ("Charlie the Weatherman" being the one that convinced me).

I asked Gabe to do some church gigs with me. He was a really talented musician, and right out of the gate he made my songs sound better. He introduced me to the music of Alison Krauss and Lyle Lovett. Over the years, we spent countless hours in the car together, listening to music by Shawn Colvin and Caedmon's Call, Jonatha Brooke and Diamond Rio, Extreme and Susan Ashton. He came up with guitar parts that I turned into songs. He wrote beautiful background vocal lines. The very fact of his friendship gave me the courage I needed back then to walk out on the stage and play Sunday evening concerts for snowbirds in Florida.

After Jamie, he was the first person to hear a new song, the first to help me work it out, the first to perform it with me. He moved to Nashville not long after Jamie and I did, and we toured together for five mostly-wonderful years. He's all over my first two albums. In short, he *resonated* with me, and I with him.

Later on, my brother Pete encouraged me in the same way, as did Ben Shive, Andy Gullahorn, Jill Phillips, Eric Peters, Andrew Osenga, Silers Bald, Laura Story, and Caedmon's Call. When I wanted to quit, it was my membership in that community of songwriters that stood me up, brushed off my knees, and helped me to believe that music was worth fighting for. And many times I did the same for them. I was a small fish in a big songwriting pond, and it was from them that I learned habits of being (thank you, Flannery), the writing life (thank you, Annie Dillard), and what it meant to stumble along in pursuit of a calling.

There was a profound sense that we were all in it together. That sense culminated for me in a meeting at Andrew Osenga's house in the early 2000s. The meeting was called because we were all trying to find our place in Nashville, trying to figure out what it looked like to be a Christian who was an artist in a post-Rich Mullins, post-9/11 world.

What, you may ask, does 9/11 have to do with anything?

I moved to Nashville in 1997, a skinny kid with long hair, a delightfully adventurous wife, and a bunch of songs. We packed up the U-Haul in Florida and drove up with a few thousand dollars saved up mostly from Jamie's teaching job. Rent was $500 a month, which was a serious stretch, and we only had about a month of savings. The pressure was on. She got a job as a part-time sitter and I got a job at that bastion of Italian culture, The Olive Garden—my first and only job as a waiter, thank God. When I wasn't serving, Jamie and I spent our days printing out press kits on our fancy color printer and mailing them. The kit included a list of recommendations from ministers in Florida, a short bio, and a headshot of me wearing a beret backwards. I also included my independent EP *Walk*, which was more or less awful. We sent out package after package to churches all over America, and I'd follow up with a call to the church secretary, using every ounce of my pastor's kid charm to try and secure a concert.

I was willing to play for a love offering. I was willing to drive unreasonable distances. I was willing to play during picnics. I was even, Lord help me, willing to play church lock-ins. After a long day of failing at waiting tables, I'd spend my meager tip money on an appetizer and bring it home for our dinner. Jamie and I would eat it while watching the comedic double-header of *Mad About You* followed by *Seinfeld*. Then I would use my dial-up AOL account to try to scour the Internet of the late nineties for possible gigs and contacts.

After weeks of trying, I couldn't get a single gig. We could always head back to Florida (a twelve-hour drive) and play at churches that already knew me, but the whole point of moving to Nashville was to try to expand the ministry. It was discouraging. Finally, I got past the gatekeeper secretary at a church somewhere in Missouri and actually got to talk to the pastor, the big cheese. I told him what I did, offered to send him my press kit, and asked if they'd be interested in a concert.

"We don't really do concerts," he said doubtfully, "but we are having a homecoming picnic in September. I guess if you wanted to come play under a tree while folks ate, that would be fine. I can't pay you, though."

"That's no problem, sir. Thank you, sir."

"Just check back with my secretary in a few weeks and she can give you the details and directions."

Yes, directions. This was before GPS. This was when the only way to get around was with a big Rand McNally atlas. This was also before cell phones, which meant that if we got lost we had to pull over to a pay phone and use a phone card with a two-hundred-digit number that I had memorized.

I hung up after offering profuse thanks, and shouted to Jamie in the other room, "We got a gig! Jamie, we got a gig!"

She burst into the room. "Really?"

"Yes. In Missouri. Should be about a seven-hour drive. We'll be singing under a tree during a picnic. For free."

We were elated.

About a week before the "show" I called the church for the details. The pastor picked up. "Did my secretary not call you?"

"No, sir."

"Well, I'm really sorry, but the board decided it wasn't really going to work to have a guy playing music during the picnic. Good luck, though!"

I'm not making this up. The one gig we were able to land had just fallen through, so I hung up the phone and stood there in my Olive Garden apron, wondering what in the world I was thinking moving my sweet wife all the way to Nashville. Who was I kidding?

That night after work, I came home and kicked off my alfredo-stained shoes, signed into AOL, and went to the website of a band I had just heard of, some Texas group named Caedmon's Call. Their music was passionate and beautiful and acoustic-ish and like nothing I'd ever heard before—the icing on the cake was that they had covered a Rich Mullins song called "Hope to Carry On." At the time they had a message board and one of the band members was active on it, replying to fans on a regular basis. I posted a short message that went something like, "Hey. My name's Andrew and I just wanted to say that I love your music. You guys' songs move me in the same way Rich's do. I'm a songwriter, and here's a link to my website where you can read my lyrics."

I surfed elsewhere for a few minutes and then headed back to the message board. The band member had responded. And he hadn't just responded. He had visited my website and told all his fans to go check out this Andrew Peterson guy's writing. I got goose bumps. Encouragement had struck like lightning.

Someone out there who hadn't even heard a note of my music was telling people that my lyrics were good. I woke Jamie up and told her the news. She wasn't surprised, because that is her way. Her answer was probably something like, "That's really cool. But of course he likes your lyrics—how could he not? Good night." She is faithful and loyal and followed me to Nashville without hesitation, not trusting me, necessarily, but trusting that God had called me to this and that we would be fine.

About two weeks later, Caedmon's Call had a show in Chattanooga, so we drove the two hours down on the off chance that we might be able to talk to them. After their show, which was wonderful, I bumped into the band and introduced myself. They remembered me from the message board and invited Jamie and I to dinner. It was surreal, especially after the depths of discouragement I had been drowning in just weeks earlier. I took a deep breath and said, "I've heard you guys let independent acts open for you sometimes. Do you think maybe I could meet you guys at the Union University show in Jackson next week and play a few songs to open?"

To my shock, Cliff Young stepped away from the table, made a call to their manager from the Friday's pay phone, came back a few minutes later, and said, "Sure."

It's hard to convey the sense of providence we felt on the drive back to Nashville that night. After all, the band hadn't even heard me sing. They hadn't listened to my album. They just said, "Yes." I still can hardly believe it—especially now, knowing what I know of how hard those guys can be to nail down. There's no doubt in my mind that God himself intervened and kicked open that door.

Later we drove to Jackson, two hours in the other direction, with my guitar and two boxes containing sixty CDs. Our rent was due and we truly had no idea how we were going to pay it. If we could sell a handful of albums we might get close. The band welcomed us graciously, got us sound-checked (breathing a sigh of relief, no doubt, that I didn't *totally* stink), and we did the show in the student union building for about five hundred students. They went bonkers after every song. We sold out of CDs in minutes, partly because Cliff told the crowd to support us. Can you believe what I'm telling you? We made six hundred dollars—enough to cover our rent. It blew my mind. We drove home elated, stopping only to splurge on some McDonald's burgers and to switch drivers at a remote rest area. When we pulled sleepily into the apartment at 2:00 a.m. and unloaded the car I asked Jamie where the money bag was. She had no idea. We looked everywhere, to no avail.

"But we paid for the McDonald's out of the money bag," I said in a panic. "I know we had it when we left. And we drove straight home, right? It has to be here."

Jamie cringed. "We switched drivers."

"What?"

"We stopped at that rest area outside of Jackson and switched drivers. It must have fallen out."

She was right. We had done the switch on the on-ramp at the rest area, which meant the bag was likely in the middle of the road, right under a streetlamp. I hung my head, trying to wake up my brain enough to make a decision.

"I have to go back," I said.

"But there's no way it'll still be there," she said.

"It's our rent. I have to try."

She went to bed and I drove two hours back to Jackson, slapping myself in the face to stay awake. I passed the rest area, got off at the next exit to turn around, and drove back to the eastbound side, infuriated at the futility of it all.

But there it was. A bright blue money bag in the middle of the ramp, in a perfect pool of light from the streetlamp above. It had sat there for four hours, untouched. *Four hours.*

I got home at 6:00 a.m. as the sun was rising.

I was wide awake.

The Jackson show went well enough that Caedmon's Call allowed me to open for them several more times that fall, at shows from Kankakee to Wheaton to Houston to College Station, Texas. It was just before the Texas run that we got the news that Rich Mullins had died in a car accident in Illinois. One of my favorite memories from that tour was a show at the Dixie Theater near Texas A&M, days after Rich's passing. Back then Caedmon's Call always ended their shows with "Hope to Carry On," kindly giving me the "I can see Peter" verse of it to sing. Their grief was different from mine; they had lost a friend. I hadn't ever spent time with Rich, but I had lost a hero—as well as the possibility of getting to know him myself just as my career was finding its legs and the chances of us crossing paths were increasing by the day. "Hope to Carry On" was more poignant that night than ever, of course, and the crowd felt it too. Cliff got the crowd started on "I See You" and we all left the stage, standing in the alleyway behind the venue and holding back tears as the crowd sang all the verses a capella.

And when that song ended they sang, spontaneously and without direction, "Step by Step," just like on the record.

The band had printed up special T-shirts for that show, and I still have mine, twenty years later.

When I got home from that trip I triumphantly turned in my resignation at Olive Garden. I was the worst waiter in the history of restaurants, so they wished me luck and went back to their cheese grinders.

Not only had Caedmon's Call given me thousands of new listeners, we sold a crazy amount of CDs. This was before iTunes. Before iPods. Before Napster. If you wanted to listen to music, and you weren't a computer nerd who knew the dirty underbelly of the Internet, you had to buy CDs. Not only that, all those college kids went home to the four corners of America on break and told their friends about the bands they had discovered. All those years—good years, mind you—of playing Sunday-night church services and youth conferences in Florida, and I had no idea there was this prime audience of college students at universities all over the country who actually liked singer-songwriter folk music and had their parents' money to spend on CDs.

Things were so different then.

The following spring, in 1998, Caedmon's Call, in another act of grace, invited me to open for their upcoming fifty-city tour. *Fifty shows.* This time, we wouldn't have to follow them around in our Ford Explorer, but would be allowed to ride in one of the two tour buses. And we didn't have to pay them. (Again, I can hardly believe it now, looking back. Such kindness.) The only catch, which wasn't really a catch at all, was that there would be another opener on the tour—some guy named Bebo Norman, who, judging by his name, was probably a blues player.

The tour was mostly magical. Other than the fact that our bus hit a donkey in the middle of the Nevada desert, things went smoothly—more than smoothly, since Bebo was wonderful and Caedmon's Call was at their apex. The crowds were all passionate and all big. Most of the shows sold out, some of them up to three thousand people. When I got home from that tour, we had enough money to order more CDs, we had a great database of fans—and we had a baby on the way.

Aedan was born in 1998, a year after Rich Mullins died, on Rich's birthday. At first I had a hard time admitting that I named him after the song "Let Mercy Lead," but it's been twenty years now, so I can come clean. He also was named after the main character in Stephen Lawhead's *Byzantium*, which I was reading when Jamie was pregnant, but the fact that he was born on Rich's birthday was significant.

Just a year after that depressing phone call with the pastor in Missouri, I found that getting shows was no longer a problem. Even if the people I called had never heard of me, they had probably heard of Caedmon's Call. But most of the shows over the next few years were returns to colleges we had played on that 1998 tour. Not only that, thanks again to Caedmon's Call, I signed my first record deal with a new label called Watershed Records. Another year later, and I was about to release my first official album, *Carried Along*. It sold really well, thanks in part to the fact that my first single, "Nothing to Say," broke the top ten (probably because I deleted the prechoruses).

Then my second son was born: Asher, named after Chaim Potok's *My Name Is Asher Lev*, which I was reading when Jamie was pregnant. (Are you catching a theme here?) We hit the road with two babies, just over a year apart—first in a Ford Explorer, then a conversion van named Junior, then in an RV we called the Millennium Falcon. How in the world did Jamie do it? I have no idea. Some nights, the boys literally slept in a suitcase. We would get to the hotel room late at night, dump out our clothes, and she would make a nest in the suitcase. When we look back at the pictures from those days we cringe. We usually looked exhausted and a little sad. There are good memories sparkling among all the weariness, but if I had to do it all over I'm not sure we'd put our kids (or our marriage) through it all.

Things were different then. I keep saying this, but it's true. The world was different. And the thing that seems to mark the change is 9/11.

My second record, *Clear to Venus*, released that very day in 2001. First it was the gut-wrenching sadness we felt for the victims and their families. Then the economy tanked. People were scared of big crowds and just didn't go to concerts. But we were on tour and we had bills to pay, so we had to do the shows even if no one came. And few people did. Just as the economy began to struggle and people were starting to pay more attention to their wallets, Napster became a house-hold name. Suddenly it was easy to steal music. I remember students coming up to me in line with illegal burned CD-Rs of my album and asking me to sign them. Shameless. Every CD they didn't buy was $15 I didn't have for diapers. Soon the record labels started shuttering, consolidating, downsizing. I'm not proud of letting myself worry as much as I did, but it happened.

Between albums two and three, my daughter Skye was born. (We named her Autumn Skye because she was born on the first day of autumn under one of the most beautiful, crisp Tennessee skies you can imagine—also I had recently spotted on a map the Isle of Skye off the coast of Scotland and was captivated by its lyrical, fairy-tale name.) After the low sales of *Love & Thunder*, my third record, which, to be fair, Watershed didn't really have to let me make because of the commercial bomb that was *Clear to Venus*, I got the fated phone call that I was being dropped.

Oh, how I wished Rich Mullins were still alive, just to have someone to talk to. I didn't want to be worried about money. I wanted to be a barefoot vagabond musician who laughed his way through trouble and sang about Jesus to whomever would listen. But when you have a wife and three babies, you can't just *not* think about money. I needed to pay the mortgage. I needed to pay for diapers, formula, shoes, electricity. And at the same time there was this calling, this vocation, which as far as I could tell hadn't changed. The songs were still coming. People were still responding to them. I felt God's pleasure while I was singing them. And then one day I got a phone call from the head of the label.

He said, "Andrew, I have two things I want to talk to you about. First, and I'm sorry to say this, but in light of the sales of your latest album, we're not going to renew your contract for the next two. Second, I know you've been talking about writing a book—a fantasy novel, wasn't it? I spoke to a literary agent named Don who's interested, and I'd love to connect you two."

Even though I could tell he was throwing me a bone with the book contact, it was a kind gesture and I appreciated it. (As a side note, Don ended up being my agent and helped secure the publishing deal with Waterbrook/Random House for *On the Edge of the Dark Sea of Darkness*, so it was a very good bone the label threw.) But in the moment I was devastated.

It never feels good to fail. Even if I knew all the Sunday school answers—answers I actually believed, by the way—the truth was, a bunch of people who believed in my music did a lot of work and put a lot of money on the line to try and sell it, and there was something about it that just fell flat somehow. I wasn't a valuable enough commodity to keep on the roster. Radio stations played a lot of my first two or three singles, then the winds changed and (with a few exceptions) they just sort of stopped playing my songs. I can still remember the brick-in-the-gut feeling I had when the call was over, the eerie, foreboding sense that something significant had just happened which would alter the shape of my life.

Here's what I didn't tell you about that phone call.

For years I had badgered the label to let me record *Behold the Lamb of God*, and for years they had said no. Finally they wrote me out of the contract for it, saying that they didn't want it, and it wouldn't count as one of the required albums on my contract but if I wanted to find the money myself and release it independently, I could. The day I was dropped from the label I was standing in Osenga's backyard while he and Ben were in the basement studio recording electric guitars on "So Long Moses."

I hung up the phone, took a deep breath, wiped a tear from my eye, and walked back into the studio. The guys were probably laughing at something and didn't notice at first that my face was pale.

"I just got dropped from my label," I told them.

They stopped laughing and offered their condolences. Then after a few moments of silence someone said, "So about this guitar part. Do you want it to come in at the top of the chorus?"

And we were off and running. It was God's kindness to me that I was not only in the middle of a project and had so much work to do that there was no time to wallow in self-pity, but I was surrounded by friends, by community, by people who told me implicitly by their involvement in my life and work that this was still worth doing, label or no label. It felt so good to walk back into that basement, roll up my sleeves, and try to craft an album about Jesus.

That's community. They look you in the eye and remind you who you are in Christ. They reiterate your calling when you forget what it is. They step into the garden and help you weed it, help you to grow something beautiful.

So someone—I think it was Jeremy Casella—called the aforementioned meeting at Osenga's house in Crieve Hall. (Weird how much of this story revolves around that house.) Most of us in the room had either been dropped by a label, had been courted and then abandoned by a label, or had experienced a wave of success and then foundered to the point of drowning. We were looking for commiseration, for solidarity, for encouragement, for tangible ways we could help one another. In a city full of songwriters, we had found kinship not so much because our music was similar (it wasn't, except in the broadest sense), but because our callings were. Once again, Rich Mullins came to mind. It would have been so nice if this man, whose music had gotten our attention years before we had met each other, who had blazed the trail we were trying, each in our own way, to follow, could have given us some wisdom and direction. But we were on our own.

I mentioned the timing of 9/11 and Napster, but there's one other factor that played at least some part in leading us all to that room: worship music. I don't know why, but sometime in the early 2000s people started going bonkers for worship music. Radio started playing it more and more, leaving less and less room for songs with any kind of narrative or grit or—dare I say it?—personality. Every band, it seemed, had a worship album in the queue. And since radio, which sometimes doesn't want to admit that it's a tastemaker, was pushing that kind of music across the airwaves of America, churches were becoming less interested in non-worship artists. The thing is, as Christians who were singer-songwriters, we were already on the fringes of things: we were too explicitly Christian in content to get much work in the club circuit, and since we were storyteller-singer-songwriters without radio hits or worship songs, it was getting harder to do church concerts.

It seemed we had three choices: (1) become more main-stream; (2) become more CCM or worship-ish; or (3) stay the course and keep writing the kinds of songs we believed in, songs like the ones that moved us, songs that were honest and open about the whole of our lives, which meant we were sometimes frank about the work of Jesus, but we weren't going to try and make them more "Christian," which meant writing songs for corporate worship just to sell records or get radio play. And the only way we could see that third option working was to lock arms with one another in community. That meant doing shows together as often as possible. If one person had a show and an opener was an option, we'd bring another friend along. If we were interviewed, we'd try and mention our friends. Jill Phillips came up with the name "The Square Peg Alliance," and we put up a website with all of our pictures and links to our websites. We sang on each other's albums. We put out a sampler CD. Suddenly, label or no label, radio or no radio, we *belonged* to something, and that something was each other. We were no longer alone. Perhaps most important, it meant that whenever I was discouraged, I had friends who gave me courage. If I wanted to quit, someone was there to look me in the eye and tell me my songs mattered, to them if not to the masses. (Remember C. S. Lewis telling Tolkien to keep writing?)

Art nourishes community.

15

COMMUNITY NOURISHES ART

L ast year I was telling someone how sad it is that I see so little of that Square Peg Alliance gang these days. Everybody's so busy that the only time we really get together is the Behold the Lamb tour each year. And then I realized that the reason we're all so busy is because we're touring and making albums, raising our kids, using our gifts for the Kingdom.

The alliance worked.

For the record, I'm not bashing the worship music craze. Some really great songs have come from it, and I've been edified and moved by some of them in church. The problem is that the sound has become so ubiquitous that many people think there's no other Christian music out there. If they don't like what they hear on Christian radio they assume they won't like any music that could be described as Christian. Meanwhile, there are so many other artists out there working just as hard at their craft, writing wonderful songs, playing in living rooms and colleges and even churches. I don't know the answer. I just wish there was a way to broadcast that music to a wider audience. I want the world to know about these folks because I believe their music is powerful and profound, and can find its way deeply into peoples' hearts—like a round peg in a round hole.

The Rabbit Room grew out of this desire to draw attention to good work that sometimes goes unnoticed. First there was music, like that of the artists I mentioned above. We wanted to make a website that would function as a hub, so that if you went online to buy a Jill Phillips CD, her site sent you to The Rabbit Room store with all the other artists she was friends with. Cross-pollination. But it was also books. There are too many good writers out there who are mostly unknown. The Rabbit Room store also carried books by Lewis, Tolkien, Marilynne Robinson, Dorothy Sayers, Flannery O'Connor, Walter Wangerin Jr., Jeffrey Overstreet, George MacDonald, and G. K. Chesterton—authors half of which you probably won't find in a typical Christian bookstore.

My friend N. D. Wilson was teaching once, and he asked the class to name some adjectives that describe Christian art. We said words like "mediocre," "cheesy," "shallow," "trite," "saccharine," and "derivative." He wrote them on the board, and the class nodded smugly. Then he reminded us that he didn't specify *modern American* Christian art. What if we answered that question with people in mind like J. S. Bach, Tolkien, Rembrandt, Carravagio, and George Herbert? The adjectives change, don't they? And for that matter, I would argue that even modern American art by Christians is *far* from cheesy and trite—if you're looking in the right place.

Not long ago a lovely video surfaced online, thanks to producer David Taylor, featuring a conversation between Bono and the late Eugene Peterson in which they discuss the Psalms over coffee. Those two are wise and humble (yes, humble), and have good things to say about the gospel and art. The film is beautifully done. But one little moment ruffled my feathers. Bono, speaking off-the-cuff about the gut-wrenching honesty of the Psalms, said that he wished Christian songwriters were that honest today. A lot of people in the comments agreed, using many of the aforementioned adjectives to brush aside all Christian music as a waste of time. This hit close to home, for obvious reasons.

I tweeted something like, "I get where Bono is coming from, but the truth is, there's TONS of honest and beautiful Christian art." I know many Christian songwriters who have written deft and devastatingly beautiful lyrics about divorce, depression, loneliness, doubt, and anger. The problem isn't that there aren't artists emulating the psalmists' honesty. The problem is that *no one seems to pay any attention to them*.

Since the Christian music industry is, after all, an industry, making money is part of their *modus operandi*. They make what sells. You can't really fault them for it. Radio stations play what keeps people listening, and therefore what keeps their lights on. It's kind of like Walmart. If nobody went there, Walmart would go out of business—so we can't put all the blame on the industry. Customers just seem to prefer something other than what Bono is talking about, so the industry follows suit. I used to rail against that kind of stuff. To my thinking, the Kingdom ought to operate differently than Walmart, so why not play songs that are deeper, *more* honest, *more* artful than everything else out there? But I realized years ago that griping did little good.

So instead of trying to change an industry that will never change, I decided to keep my head down and focus on what I'm called to. It meant not writing songs just for radio, but also celebrating when they decided to add my songs now and then to their playlists. They're not the enemy, after all, and radio does a lot of good for a lot of people. It also meant trying to think of other ways to draw attention to the good and true and beautiful works of art that are being made by Christians—hence, The Rabbit Room.

It's been more than ten years now, and I like to think our little ministry has done some good work. People have discovered new songwriters, new authors, new artists. But perhaps more important, they've also discovered new friends. Art just seems to draw people together. C. S. Lewis famously said that friendship is born in that moment when one person says to another, "You too? I thought I was the only one."[9] After a few years of The Rabbit Room blog, which featured essays by authors, pastors, songwriters, and artists, we realized that the readers and commenters were forming into a community—as were the writers, many of whom didn't know each other at first. My brother Pete and I cooked up a plan to host a conference, a sort of living, breathing version of what was happening on the website, just to see what would happen.

Church of the Redeemer is a lovely little Anglican church in Nashville where Fr. Thomas McKenzie, one of The Rabbit Room contributors, is the pastor. They let us use their building, which isn't modern and frilly at all, but is beautiful and tastefully decorated. (The sanctuary was hung with the Stations of the Cross, as well as a gorgeous painting of the Resurrection.) We made it clear to the registrants that this was *not* a workshop, which meant it wouldn't be appropriate to bring demos for critique or to "network" for a publishing deal. For that

---

9. C. S. Lewis, *The Four Loves* (Nashville: HarperOne; Reissue Edition, 2017).

matter, this conference wasn't specifically for artists, but for people who resonated with art in general—which meant everyone. The sessions weren't about getting published or finding a record deal, but were rather about an array of topics celebrating and meditating on certain works or the makers of those works, and the way God speaks to us through them. We paired up speakers so the sessions would feel more like a conversation than a lecture. I remember my first session, an appreciation of George MacDonald, was with banjo player Ron Block. Another year Ben Shive and I did one on Rich Mullins. We also tried to break down the walls between attendees and leaders by having us all eat together all weekend, by involving the leaders in multiple ways so they were easily accessible, and by not having a green room where they got all chummy with each other and hid from the attendees. To be forthright, that was initially due to necessity, since the church building literally didn't have a spare room. But when we read the comment cards so many expressed surprise and appreciation that there wasn't any sense of elitism or hierarchy, so the lack of a green room stuck.

The other important ingredient that makes The Rabbit Room unique is something that's become a bone of contention I like to gnaw on. A few years ago I noticed that people had made a noun out of the word *creative*, as in, "If you're a creative, aren't you sick of people not understanding that normal rules don't apply to you?" The first few times I read about "being a creative" I leaned into it and thought, "Yes. That's what I am. I'm a creative." It was subtle and seductive. And then I noticed, possibly because of the Holy Spirit, that I felt *proud* of it, which led to a sense of disdain for people who weren't like me. (For the record, I realize this is a problem with my own heart, but I doubt I'm alone in this.)

Now there are conferences for "creatives," and it just won't go away. It took me a while to figure out what irritated me about it, but it comes down to this: we're *all* creative. There is no "creative class." Sure, there are people who make their living as artists and entrepreneurs. But those people, I insist, are no more creative than anyone else. Lewis and Tolkien, you won't be surprised to know, spoke to both the sinful allure of being a part of an Inner Ring and the inherent creativity of all people. (Read "The Inner Ring" by Lewis and "On Fairy Stories" by Tolkien.)

In Tolkien's essay he argues that one of the ways we bear the image of a Creator God is that we are compelled to create. In Tolkien's case, he built Middle-earth and invented languages, writing in his poem "Mythopoeia," that "we make still by the law in which we're made." To say that my wife, who would be the first to tell you she isn't an artist, isn't creative, is to me an offensive thought. She gave birth to three children, and there's nothing on earth more beautifully creative than that. Also, our house is lovely, and it always smells good. She has laid down her life to create a nurturing, welcoming, hospitable place for our children to grow up. Don't tell me she's not creative.

So, one guiding principle of The Rabbit Room is that it's not just for artists—it's for *everyone*. Hutchmoot, as the conference came to be known, now has the tagline, "A conference for everyone." Our hope from the beginning is that it would encourage people to look for the glimmer of the gospel in all corners of life, that they would see their God-given creativity in both their artistic works and their front gardens, in their home repair and the making of their morning coffee, and that they would call out that glorious creativity in everyone they meet.

Anyone who was there for the first Hutchmoot will attest to the fact that something special happened. The conversations were rich, the food delicious, the music and readings excellent, and in the end we knew we had experienced the birth of something beautiful. I usually describe it as incarnation. The Rabbit Room existed exclusively online, and then one day it put on flesh. The blog was the lyrics, but the conference was the day the song was first sung. Community, you see, doesn't really exist online. It wants to happen in person, over a meal, during a conversation, where two or more are gathered in God's name.

Suddenly there were people from all over the country raising toasts together to celebrate the existence of good stories and songs and the way God speaks to us through them. Pete and I looked around that first year in awe, observing the embodiment of what we'd been writing about and dreaming of for years. People became friends; people experienced a sort of living, breathing art; the gospel was proclaimed; artists of all sorts were encouraged to keep making, because in making by the law in which they're made, they're pushing back at the darkness, at the lie that says, "Step aside, you non-creatives, and leave the artistic stuff to us professionals."

Of the many things I love about Hutchmoot, one is that there are regulars, folks who show up every year, some of whom have become good friends. I don't want to oversell it, though. We've goofed up plenty, and are always trying to let it grow organically while fighting to preserve the intimacy that makes it special. Some moots have been better than others. We're grappling with the usual questions a nonprofit organization has to grapple with. But there's no question in my mind that God is doing something beautiful and unique in this community, something we all feel blessed to be a part of and are doing our best to steward.

The very first year, though, someone asked a certain question during a panel, and that question has dogged us ever since. The question was this: "You guys keep talking about community, and it's clear that you have a great one. But what about the rest of us? What about me? How am I supposed to do this back home?"

Part of the reason we can afford to bring in such an abundance of guest speakers and artists at Hutchmoot is that they already live in Nashville. Attendees travel from the four corners of the country (and often from outside the U.S.) to our lovely city, and when they experience this odd little community of Christians who love the arts, they think, "If I lived in Nashville my life would be amazing." But that's not really the answer, is it?

When I met Wendell Berry and told him that after I read *Jayber Crow*, I sold my house and moved to the country, his wife Tanya said, "Oh, boy. You're not one of *those* are you?" Wendell sighed and said, "People tell us all the time that they want to move to Kentucky. That's not what I *mean*. The point is to love where you are."

I assured him that I only moved about three miles, so no, I wasn't one of "those" people. (I conveniently left out the part about how I researched property in Kentucky before we decided to stay in Nashville.)

When people say they've "found a home" with The Rabbit Room community I gently push back and say, "This isn't meant to be your home. It's a wayside inn." Frodo didn't stay in Lothlorien. Lucy had to go back to England. And that's where things get tricky. The question dogs me because I don't really have a practical answer. The obvious one is that the community you've been given is the one you have to learn to love. It's going to look different than Nashville, so let it speak to you, just like a song you're trying to write—let it become what it wants to become. Serve the work, remember?

Ah, but that makes it sound so easy. Several years back, a music minister picked me up at the airport on a Sunday morning and drove me to soundcheck for a service I was playing. He was *way* into worship music, and he said, "Man, you're so lucky to live in Nashville with all those musicians. I bet the worship there is, like, *awesome*." I took the opportunity to soapbox about how it's not about how good the musicians are. Worship shouldn't hinge on how good the band is, you know? The people on his music team were the people God had brought to that community. It sounds so wise, right? I was pleased with myself for offering up such a sage and loving rebuke. Then I got to the church and sat on the front pew, waiting for the music team to finish rehearsing so I could soundcheck, and let me tell you—they were terrible. I don't mean to be snooty, but it was hard not to cringe. And I thought to myself, "Man, I'm lucky to live in Nashville with all those musicians. The worship there is, like, *awesome.*"

It was a humbling moment. I have banished myself from that soapbox. It really is a complicated question.

The truth is, it really is nice to go to a church where the music is tastefully played. And if you're an artist and you live in a town without a ton of good musicians or poets or novelists, there's going to be a struggle. At the same time, I happen to think that if you start doing the work of joyfully, diligently speaking light into your community with your gifting, people will show up, just like in *Field of Dreams.* I've said it before: there have always been poets underfoot. God just keeps making them. So keep your eyes peeled. People will surprise you with their gifts. And you'll see how the friendships are augmenting everyone's talent in one way or another.

On the other hand, isn't there something deeply beautiful about people like Hilda Mallard, who faithfully played piano and organ at my church for about three hundred years, who taught piano lessons, who was among the first to arrive every Sunday morning and evening, and who had no aspirations to a career in music? She had a gift. She served with it. True story: my wife Jamie also had no aspirations for a music career, but she played piano for chapel in college, and at her home church on Sundays. She had a gift. She served with it. It's partly why I fell in love with her. It's why her church did, too.

The closest thing to a real answer to this question happened in November of 2018. I was on the Christmas tour, weary from a long season of travel, discouraged because I was spearheading a capital campaign to raise money for a renovation of North Wind Manor, The Rabbit Room's farm-house headquarters. We had a *long* way to go to meet our goal, and I had no idea how we were going to do it. I felt very alone. Then I flipped open my computer and saw on The Rabbit Room's Facebook page that author Rebecca Reynolds had come up with a lovely idea:

"I want a Hymnmoot. Just hours and hours of singing hymns together. Nothing complicated. Just a church, a bunch of real hymnals, and some people who are musical enough to get us going. . . . This would be a really cool fundraiser for North Wind Manor."

Literally minutes later artist Stephen Crotts had created a beautiful banner image for everyone to share. And the comments piled on. "I'll do one in East Tennessee!" "I can host one in central North Carolina." "My house in Wisconsin is open." "I collect hymnals!" On and on it went, and I'm not ashamed to tell you I had tears in my eyes. The community rallied behind the idea in the most beautiful way. In the end, on November 30, without any direction from The Rabbit Room staff, the community organized *thirty-five* simultaneous hymn sings around the country, from Minnesota to Pennsylvania to Kansas to Colorado to Ohio. They ate pie, prayed together, and sang praises to our God. It was an overwhelming affirmation of the ministry, not just because of the gesture of solidarity but because it proved that you can do this stuff right now, wher-ever you live, no matter how, like, *awesome* the musicians are. As hundreds of friends new and old gathered around a shared love for the gospel, music, and each other, Hymnmoot profoundly demonstrated that community—especially Christ-centered community—nourishes art, and art nourishes community.

Rumor has it, Hymnmoot's going to be a yearly thing. Like Rebecca said in that original post, all you need is some people musical enough to get you going. What are you waiting for?

16

HOME IS REAL

In the summer of 2016 my family and I traveled to Europe to play music. Our eldest, Aedan, was about to be a senior in high school, which meant the following summer he would likely be preoccupied with college, so we planned one last Peterson family adventure before life as we knew it changed. That trip was wonderful in so many ways, chief among them the time spent with friends we've made over the years in Sweden and the United Kingdom. First we flew to Stockholm and traveled the fair country of Sweden, performing several times as a family band and consuming the finest desserts (and the strongest coffee) you can imagine. Midsummer in Sweden is a joyous affair, when little girls make wreaths out of wildflowers and wear them like fairy crowns. Because of the high latitude the sunsets last for hours, and even at midnight there's still a glow in the west. My ancestors were Swedes, so I feel an ancient sense of belonging when I'm there, a sense made all the more poignant because of the friends and distant relatives we've come to know over the years.

Right before my first tour in Sweden I called my dad.

"Dad, we're Swedish, right?"

He laughed. "Yeah, my grandfather emigrated from there to Amherst, Massachusetts."

"Do you know where he was from? What was his name?"

"His name was Ernest, but they used to spell it 'Ernst.' According to my records, he came from a city called Kalmar."

My first time there I bashfully told a few Swedes this information and to my surprise they were interested. In Gamla Stan ("Old Town") Stockholm, among the shops on one of the narrow cobbled alleyways, I found a place that sold old prints and bought a couple of nineteenth-century pictures of the Castle Kalmar, which I framed and hung on the wall when I got home. "This," I told my children when I got home, "is a real castle, in the same city where your great-great-grandfather used to live. Get this: there's a good chance he rode a horse past this castle." It captured my imagination, and I hope it captured theirs.

As I said, because I was born in Illinois, in a little town with no other family, when we moved I lost any real claim on the place. And when we settled in a small southern Florida town where most of the people had been there for generations, I always felt like an outsider there, too. We've been in Nashville for more than twenty years, longer than I've ever lived anywhere—and yet, it's still just a place I chose. We made a life here, and I'm grateful for it, but it's my children's hometown, not mine. I've always ached to belong somewhere. I think it's part of why so many of my songs are about the New Creation. So when I found out the Petersons were so recently connected to Sweden, land of Vikings and reindeer and cool furniture, I latched onto it. Is *this my home?* I wondered as I walked those streets the first time. I felt a tug in my heart whenever I looked at the etching of that old castle.

Not long after that first trip I joined one of those ancestry websites and got to work on the Peterson family tree. To say I was interested is a massive understatement. I was obsessed.

HOME IS REAL

Over the years, usually a few weeks before a tour in Sweden, I
would renew my membership to the website and scour histor-
ical records for information about my family. Surely, if Ernst
had siblings who never emigrated, I still had distant Swedish
cousins.

One of my dreams, after a few tours there, was to bring
my whole family so they could meet the friends I'd made and
walk the land our forefathers had walked. In 2013 it finally
happened, partly because I was having a midlife crisis/depres-
sion/breakdown. My counselor asked me one day, as I sat there
crying, if in the fifteen years or so that I'd been touring I'd ever
taken a sabbatical. Of course the answer was no. Unless you're
independently wealthy, it's pretty hard to take a real break
when you're self-employed. He asked me what I'd most want
to do. "Get out of Nashville," I answered. "With my family. For
a long time." He asked where I'd want to go. "Sweden." It took
a lot of planning and saving and recklessness, but we did it.
Nine weeks in Sweden and the U.K. (The irony is, in order to
pay for it I had to play shows the whole time—but I was with
my family, and we were staying put in each place for long
enough to get some rest.)

Anyway, in anticipation of this trip I paid a Swedish guy
named Connie to do some real research, and he emailed one
day in triumph, saying that he had found my ancestral home.
Weeks later, we met Connie on a back road in the region of
Sweden near Kalmar called Småland (or, "Small Land"), which
sounds marvelously Shire-like, doesn't it? He drove us down
a gravel road through an old forest to a classic Swedish farmhouse, painted that lovely deep red. An eighty-year-old man

177

hobbled out of the house and greeted us, then directed us to a bunch of bicycles he'd borrowed from the neighbors. We biked a few miles into the forest on old, muddy paths. He told us through Connie that my great-grandfather's family had lived in a cottage in those woods, but he couldn't remember exactly where the ruins were. He kept pulling over and poking through the brush, then he'd shake his head, get back on his bike, and wave us on.

Connie explained that he was looking for a certain kind of berry that would tell him where the old foundation stones would be. A hundred years ago, he said, the berries were planted outside the cottage for food, and long after the house fell into ruin, the berry bushes lived on. If you want to find the remains of a dwelling in a Swedish forest, Connie told us, look for berries. Then at last, with a happy grunt, the old man dismounted and beckoned us off the path. We climbed through the brush as he chattered to us in Swedish, though we had indicated several times that we didn't speak it.

And there it was, surrounded by tall trees: a cellar, probably for storing potatoes, which would have been under the cottage. The big stones that lined it were green with moss, placed in a rough square about five feet across. Humus and leafy debris littered the bottom, and when I jumped in it was springy. We got our picture taken while the old man smiled on, then because the mosquitoes were vicious, we rode back. Mission accomplished. I assumed my investigation into family history was over. I had found what I was looking for, and had given my children a memory that few Americans can lay claim to.

But the story wasn't over. The next time I was in Sweden I couldn't stop wondering what had happened to the rest of my family. Every time I met a Peterson (which is pretty often over there) I wondered if we were related. So I kept digging on the websites, kept pressing my dad for more information, and every time I came back the hunt resumed.

Then, in 2016, I found them.

I emailed a woman named Ingrid, who I was certain was my grandfather's first cousin. I wrote, "You don't know me, but I'm an American singer-songwriter and I think you're my second cousin. I have a show in Uppsala this Friday, and I'd love for you to be my guest." She emailed back that day using Google Translate and said, "I thought this might be some kind of scam, but I watched some of your music videos, and I think you are telling the truth. I will see you Friday."

When she arrived at the concert I knew her immediately. She looked vaguely like my grandfather. She kissed me on the cheek and we both had tears in our eyes. Ingrid brought black-and-white pictures of her grandfather, who was my great-great grandfather. We didn't have a lot to talk about, but neither of us minded. We just sort of sat there, enjoying the resonance of our shared blood. At one point I FaceTimed my dad so they could say hello to each other. Later that year I returned with my family and Ingrid treated us to lunch in Hjälstaby, the little town where she had grown up, and where my great-great grandfather had lived at one time. We walked through the old stone church he would have attended and saw the thousand-year-old baptismal font. No joke, there was a Viking rune stone outside the church, surrounded by wild daisies.

By the end of those few weeks in Sweden we had experienced legendary hospitality in the kindness of Christians; we had seen wide fields of summer flowers and woodlands bright with linnea blooms; we had stood among ancient ruins, and were ferried to islands where ancient kings once lived; we had sung for hundreds of people about the Kingdom that is to come.

Linnea is a lovely little woodland flower that grows in the forests of Småland. The last day there, I wrote this and sang it at Gullbranna Festival.

Linnea

My father's father talked about a home
And he never laid his eyes upon these shores
But he knew it in his blood and in his bones
There must be something more

O linnea, O linnea
The grace of God is growing
In these forests and these fields
O linnea, O linnea
Home is real, home is real, home is real

Twelve years ago I took a plane to Stockholm
And I could see it in your faces like the carvings of the runes
In the steeples rising peaceful from the hills
Beneath the midsummer moon

O linnea, O linnea
The grace of God is growing
In these forests and these fields
O linnea, O linnea
Home is real, home is real, home is real

If I could see my father's father now
I'd tell him what I've seen
That he was born and he was raised in a foreign land
It's a good thing to believe
In a place you've never been
But it's a better thing to get there in the end
It's a better thing to feast there with your friends

My children now can tell the old, old story
How the holy love of Jesus in your faces was revealed
And in a thousand years that love will still be growing
Like linnea in the fields

O linnea, O linnea
The grace of God is growing
In these forests and these fields
O linnea, O linnea
Home is real, home is real, home is real
Love is real, love is real, love is real

Even after all that, I ache for home. I still yearn for a place to belong. Even with the stone arch and the cottage garden and the memories of young laughter among the low-hung trees, even as I've tasted honey the bees conjured from wild-flowers on my own land, though it was as sweet as the righteous Word of the Lord—even still, Jamie and I move through our story and sense the unfinishedness of things. As I sit in The Chapter House I can see on the wall, next to the painting of Castle Kalmar, a hundred signatures of friends who have spent time in here, and though I hold dear the remembrance of their fellowship I know their bodies are winding ever down, as mine is, to a long and expectant sleep. Though we strike out on the Christmas tour every December, my friends and I, to sing the story of the Incarnation, we carry with us a quiet hollow in the heart, an unrung bell that waits to sound with the final note of the reappearing of the Lamb of God. My brother and I continue to serve The Rabbit Room ministry, setting a table for the writers and artists, bards and wanderers who can't shake the feeling of a spiritual homesickness. We feel it too. At church, even when I receive the Eucharist and sing songs of the Good King with my friends and family, I feel that same persistent longing, dogging my every step. My heart, God help me, is restless, and has ever been so. What, Jesus, can I do?

Write about it, a voice says in my head. Tell that story.

But I get so tired. I know my heart is plagued with sin after sin after sin—sins that would appall you, dear reader—and the voice still says Write about that. Don't hold it in. Watch how even that can bring me glory.

Ah, Lord, I'm so weak! And so foolish. I've hurt my wife, my children, my friends. I just want to go home.

Write that song. Write that story. Homesickness is the way home.

One day, perhaps, when I'm dead and gone, and my songs and stories lie in the ruins of some old forest and no one remembers my name, whatever good and beautiful and human thing that the King of Creation called forth from me will fall to the earth and grow brambly and wild, and some homesick and hungry soul will leave the well-worn path and say, "Look! Someone lived here. Praise God, there are berries everywhere."

That is what I want for you.

I want you, dear reader, to remember that one holy way of mending the world is to sing, to write, to paint, to weave *new* worlds. Because the seed of your feeble-yet-faithful work fell to the ground, died, and rose again, what Christ has done through you will call forth praise from lonesome travelers long after your name is forgotten. They will know someone lived and loved here.

Whoever they were, they will think, *they belonged to God. It's clear that they believed the stories of Jesus were true, and it gave them a hope that made their lives beautiful in ways that will unfold for ages among the linnea that shimmers in the moonlit woods.*

This is why the Enemy wants you to think you have no song to write, no story to tell, no painting to paint. He wants to quiet you. So *sing*. Let the Word by which the Creator made you fill your imagination, guide your pen, lead you from note to note until a melody is strung together like a glimmering constellation in the clear sky. Love the Lord your God, and love your neighbor, too, by making worlds and works of beauty that blanket the earth like flowers. Let your homesickness keep you always from spiritual slumber. Remember that it is in the fellowship of saints, of friends and family, that your gift will grow best, and will find its best expression.

And until the Kingdom comes in its fullness, bend your will to the joyful, tearful telling of its coming.

Write about that.

Write about that, and never stop.

AFTERWORD
(NUTS AND BOLTS)

I realize that some of you aren't songwriters (or novelists or poets, for that matter). But hopefully I've made it clear that (1) we're all creative, and (2) there's a lot of similarity in process no matter what your discipline is. People always want to know what comes first, the music or the lyrics. Music is such an integral part of God's creation, evidenced in Scripture, nature, and humanity—which makes me think maybe everybody's a closet songwriter on some level. Even if you're not, I want to offer up some good old-fashioned advice. It might be helpful even if all you know how to play is the radio, as the old Dad Joke goes.

1. Don't overwrite. Keep it simple. Only use a big, fancy word or an unconventional structure if it's serving the song and loving the listener.

2. Don't obsess over the perfect rhyme. This is not an excuse to be lazy. But I think it's better to pay more attention to the aesthetic of the line, its effectiveness, how singable it is, than making sure it lines up perfectly and rhymes like Dr. Seuss. This hits on the discernment principle, because you need to make sure that if you're sacrificing the rhyme, the line actually works. You have to earn the right to break the rules.

3. Obsess over the perfect rhyme! And the perfect rhyme might be a slant rhyme, or an internal one. Constraints are wonderful things, and lead you down paths you might not otherwise take. (Yes, I know points two and three are saying two different things. Go with it.) If you choose to break the rhyme pattern, don't do it because it's too hard to make it work, but because the song calls for it.

4. Rewrite, but not too much. Revision is crucial, of course, but it's possible to monkey with something so much that the magic dies and the character is gone. It reminds me of a Rich Mullins story I heard from Michael Aukofer, one of his bandmates. Michael was tuning the hammered dulcimer in the studio, which, if you don't know anything about hammered dulcimers, is a royal pain in the rear. He had finally gotten it in tune when Rich walked by and said, "Oh, hey. Make sure you bang on that thing a lot and get it out of tune before we record it or it won't sound real."

5. Remember the Buechner Principle, which is that the story of one of us is, in some measure, the story of us all. You may think your life isn't interesting enough to write about, but, trust me, that's just not true. If you're really stuck, pick a family member and write about (or for) them. The magic is in the details, however mundane they may seem on the surface.

6. Write like other writers. If you're stuck, pick your favorite songwriter and try writing a song like her. Imagine you're writing it for her to sing. Use her tricks, her grooves, her structures. In the end, you'll have something that's reminiscent of her, but is still yours. Ask yourself, what would Sara Groves do with this piano part? How would James Taylor transition to the bridge?

7. Learn other people's songs. Sit down with your favorite songs and learn the guitar or piano parts exactly. Not only does this make you a better player, because you're practicing, but it opens up whole chambers of possibility when you see how they voice chords or move from one section of a song to another. In the book *My Name Is Asher Lev* (which you should read), the young art student has to paint and repaint the works of the masters hundreds of times before his teacher lets him paint his own.

8. Try different tunings. This is true mainly if you're a guitar player. But experimenting with odd tunings gives you different voicings that suggest different melodies which broaden your musical palette.

9. Jesu juva. I mentioned this in chapter 3, but it bears repeating. Several years ago Rabbit Room contributor Lanier Ivester wrote a post about the fact that Bach wrote "Soli Deo Gloria," or "Glory to God alone," at the bottom of his manuscripts. This is a good and beautiful thing, and I'd suggest doing the same in your notebooks. But don't forget the "Jesu juva," or "Jesus, help!" If you looked through my journals you'd see that written again and again. God is the Word that made the world, the source of all goodness, beauty, and truth. We would be fools not to invoke his aid anytime we try to speak something into being.

10. Be willing to be misunderstood. This might fly in the face of the "serve the listener" principle, but I think it's a matter of calling. In *The Terrible Speed of Mercy*, Jonathan Rogers's wonderful biography of Flannery O'Connor, he writes about her willingness to tell the stories she was called to tell, even if it meant the critics and the audience sometimes missed her point entirely. She took a long view, and though it was painful, stayed true to her calling and trusted that it was God's business what he did with her stories after they were written. She wrote, "God may use my work to save some people and to test the faith of others, but that's His business and none of mine." Even if you're serving your audience well, there will be those who don't get it. Be content with that. As long as you're holding fast to that which has taken hold of you, as long as you're obedient to your gifting and your vocation, then accolades and record sales and being understood aren't any of your business. This must be held in tension with the humility of being in community with people who you'll truly listen to, who will help you to see when you need to change and when you need to stick to your guns.

11. Honesty, truth, and beauty. This, for me, is the trifecta of good Christian art, and it's exemplified in much of Rich Mullins's work. Here's what I mean. He was honest about his own doubts, his own story. He often wrote from a very human place, and peppered his songs with place names (Wichita), friends of his (Susan), and folky vernacular ("You was a baby like I was once, you was cryin' in the early morning."), but he was confessional about his inner landscape, too ("I know that I am only lashing out at the one who loves me most"). So he was honest (and by that I also mean human). He also told the truth, which is to say, his songs aimed the listener at Scripture, at God, not himself. Even as he was being honest about his struggle to believe, he was constantly aiming those doubts at the author of our faith—not only that, his prolific use of Scripture in his songs gave them a gravitas that worked in wonderful tension with the human aspect. And finally, what he wrote was beautiful. He was a gifted poet, and flexed that muscle often in songs like "The Color Green,"

"The Love of God," and "Calling Out Your Name." A song that braids those three qualities well is going to have a profound impact. If you remove just one of the three, things change. For example, a song that is honest and beautiful, but not infused with the truth of the gospel, will be like some of the excellent mainstream works out there. Josh Ritter comes to mind. His songs are dripping with beauty, and he sometimes exhibits a wonderful honesty, but he's so opposed to Christianity his songs are less than they could be. Or if you had a song that was true and beautiful, but not honest and human, you'd have hymns, or the kind of Christian music that could be sung by anybody. Again—this isn't necessarily a bad thing, but it's missing the grit of humanity, the feeling that a real person with real troubles wrote the song. Finally, if a song was true and honest, but not very pretty, you'd have the kind of stuff bad demos are made of—I've written plenty of these. If it's not beautiful (or skillful or excellent—you know what I mean), there's not much point, is there? Whether or not you agree, that's the kind of thing I'm always aiming for, and the Psalms exhibit this again and again: honesty, truth, and beauty.

12. Give them 2+2, not 4. This has as much to do with performing as songwriting, and is an idea I got from Pixar guru Andrew Stanton (who directed Wall-E and Finding Nemo). He explained in a speech I found online that this was a storytelling principle the Pixar team discovered along the way—that the audience wants to work for their entertainment, but not *too* hard. You don't treat them like they're idiots, you don't spell out every gag, every point you want them to get, or they'll get bored. They'll get the feeling you don't trust them.

People are smart, and enjoy filling in the blanks, which is what it means to "get a joke." If you have to explain it, either it was a bad joke or you didn't tell it very well. So when you're writing a song or a story, invite the audience to engage with you by not showing all your cards, by setting them up for an "aha!" moment. On the other hand, don't make them work *too* hard, or they'll check out, either because you've made them feel dumb or they just get bored. So if you're a songwriter introducing a song at a show, don't tell them what the song is about. Tell them just enough to engage them; let the song be the answer to the question you raised in your introduction. I used to introduce an old song called "Pillar of Fire," about the hard journey of faith, with a story from George MacDonald's book *The Princess and the Goblin*, in which the princess has to follow her fairy godmother's invisible thread to safety by feeling for it in the dark. When the goblins invade the castle, she finds the thread and follows, but instead of leading her deeper into the safety of the castle, it leads her out the window and into the woods, and eventually into the lair of the goblins—where in the end, counterintuitively, she finds refuge. I'd tell the story, then say, "Just thought I'd share that with you." They would laugh, because it seemed like a *non sequitur*, then I'd play "Pillar of Fire," and during the song I could see them connecting the dots. Rich Mullins used to say that what you said in between songs was just as important as the songs themselves. If you've ever heard him talk, you know what I mean.

13. Read poetry. Study poetry. Know at least something about what an iamb and a trochee and a spondee are. Words matter, phrasing matters, lines matter. Don't assume that poetry is just for snobs and grad students, because it isn't. Part of the delight of good songwriting is when it unfolds itself to you over the course of many listens, like when I realized after listening to and performing Rich Mullins's "The Color Green" many times, I discovered a subtle rhyme pattern buried in the lyrics, or when an image in verse two foreshadows another one in verse three.

14. Read books. If you're going to deal in the currency of language, then read, read, read. Be curious. Go to the library and check out more books than you have time to read, about subjects you may only have a passing interest in. You never know when or where the perfect metaphor might present itself to you. Delight in the fact that God made the world with a Word, and that the early Christians were called the People of the Book, and stories are the language our hearts were made to speak and to understand. Read! Read your Bible.

15. Find your focal practice. Arthur Boers, in his book *Living into Focus*, talks about the importance of focal practices in a world that is becoming increasingly technological. What's a focal practice? In the simplest terms, it's something that doesn't involve a computer screen. It's something that gets you outside, engages you with God's creation, gets your hands dirty. He defines a focal practice as having these criteria: (1) it demands discipline and hard work; (2) it connects us with others (and our own hearts); and (3) it puts us in touch with realities greater than ourselves. As I heard Arthur speak about this, I kept thinking, "This is why I love beekeeping." I fell into beekeeping for a bunch of reasons, but once I fell in, I went deep. In hindsight, I think it's because I spend so much of my time looking at a screen, or up in my head trying to write. Beekeeping reconnects me with God's creation, takes discipline and study and practice, gave me new friends in my bee mentors, and allows my heart to soar with wonder at the way God made the world. The same could be said of gardening. I can't overstate how important it is to find something that meets these criteria, whether it's hiking, biking, carpentry, or gardening—anything that reminds you that the world is real and it is brimming with God's presence. This can only help your writing.

ACKNOWLEDGMENTS

I'm so grateful to Devin Maddox and the team at B&H for helping me shape this barrage of thoughts and anecdotes into an actual book. It's an honor to work with you all.

I dedicated this book to Christie Bragg, but it bears mentioning again that she's been a tremendous blessing to my family over the years, along with her amazing team at Bragg Management—which includes Ashley Bayne, Cara Fox, Todd Bragg, and about a zillion other assistants and interns over the years who have helped with everything from water bottles at concerts to plane tickets to scheduling and contracts and emails and everything in between.

If you've followed The Rabbit Room blog over the years, you may have found some portions of this book familiar. A few of the chapters were reworked from essays I've written over the years. The chapter "The Integrated Imagination" first appeared in volume one of The Molehill, The Rabbit Room's yearly literary journal. If, on the other hand, these ideas are new to you, this is a good time to encourage you to check out the mountain of essays and podcasts and resources written by the good people in our community, all available at www.RabbitRoom.com. And if you want to support our work, consider becoming a full-fledged, card-carrying member.

Thanks to my brother, writing mentor, and tastemaker, A. S. "Pete" Peterson, who's such a good novelist/playwright/poet that I'm honestly intimidated by the thought of him reading this book. Hopefully he'll just skip to the acknowledgments.

Thanks to Heidi Johnston and Kenny Woodhull for their wonderful feedback on an early draft. Heidi told me that it made her want to finish *her* next book, which was the most encouraging thing she could have said. Ben Shive and Andy Gullahorn taught me more about songwriting (and friendship) than anyone in the world. Thanks, Captains.

There are too many names to list, but I want to acknowledge the many communities jammed with saints who have shown me far more grace than I deserve: the Square Peg Alliance, the Same Band, The Rabbit Room, and Dude Breakfast, not to mention all the dear friends and pilgrims in Sweden, Northern Ireland, England, and the rest of the U.K. and Europe.

As I've worked on this book my three children kept coming to mind as prime examples of the kind of creative life I want to live in Christ. They've taught me so much.

Aedan has been both a spiritual compass for me and a paragon of the principles I wrote about here. His visual art is marvelous, and I can't wait to see what the Lord has in store for him as he stewards the tremendous gift he's been given. As good as his art is, though, his kindness, faithfulness, gentleness, and wisdom comprise the heart that beats at the center of his work. I couldn't be prouder to be his father and his friend.

Asher works harder and complains less than anybody I know. When he was little I had a hunch that he'd be a good drummer. Now he's a grown man, and one of the best parts of my life has been sharing the stage with him night after night and realizing as I'm playing my songs that in the most wonderful reversal of roles, the dad is leaning on the son to hold the music together. He's producing records, touring with bands, and composing songs—and by doing so in community for the glory of God, he's exemplifying the thrust of this book.

Skye is a force of nature. Her faith is deep, her talent massive, and her love for people broad and Christlike. As of this publication she's seventeen and still at home, and I'm already grieving the fact that in a few years Jamie and I won't hear her singing her heart out in her bedroom at night, or unself-consciously fighting her way through a song at the piano during the day. I'm constantly finding her lyrics scribbled on random scraps of paper scattered about the house. There's nothing better than a home full of music, and she fills ours like Niagara Falls. I can't wait to see how it pours out from here into the world.

By the way, people have asked Jamie and me how we fostered their talent, and to be honest, I don't know. Maybe it's just because in our house, art was a matter of course, along with prayer and Scripture and church. We didn't force it on them. In fact, we hardly gave them any formal training (not that lessons are a bad thing). We simply treated creativity and imagination as a natural part of Christ's intention for his people, and then fanned the flame whenever our kids showed a creative spark. Oh, how I've delighted in seeing them outpace what little I could teach. As soon as I removed the training wheels, they left me in the dust, tearing through the streets of their own creativity. It's been a pleasure to watch them go.

Finally, my deepest thanks go to Jamie, whose unflagging affection has given me courage for twenty-five years now. She'd never claim to be an artist, but she's one of the most creative people I know. Her song is our family.

READING LIST

I mentioned quite a few books in the previous pages, so I thought I'd list some of them here (along with some I didn't) in case you want to dig a little deeper.

On Creative Work

Walking on Water, Madeline L'Engle

Bird by Bird, Anne Lamott

Voicing Creation's Praise, Jeremy Begbie

Creator Spirit, Steve Guthrie

On Stories, C. S. Lewis

The Writing Life, Annie Dillard

On Fairy Stories, J. R. R. Tolkien

Art in Action, Nicholas Wolterstorff

The Mind of the Maker, Dorothy Sayers

The Terrible Speed of Mercy, Jonathan Rogers

Poetic Meter and Poetic Form, Paul Fussell

A Poetry Handbook, Mary Oliver

Rules for the Dance, Mary Oliver

Beate Not the Poore Desk, Walter Wangerin Jr.

Orthodoxy, G. K. Chesterton

Telling the Truth, Frederick Buechner

Poetry

Collected Poems, Richard Wilbur

Mayflies, Richard Wilbur

Nine Horses, Billy Collins

Sailing Alone Around the Room, Billy Collins

Living Things, Anne Porter

A Timbered Choir, Wendell Berry

The Supper of the Lamb, Robert Farrar Capon

The Poems of Gerard Manley Hopkins

The Poems of George Herbert

The Collected Poems of G. K. Chesterton

The Poems of George MacDonald

The Freeing of the Dust, Denise Levertov

The Spirit Level, Seamus Heaney

Beowulf, Seamus Heaney

Poem a Day, Karen McCosker and Nicholas Albery, eds.

Good Poems, Garrison Keillor, ed.

ABOUT THE AUTHOR

Andrew is a singer, songwriter, author, filmmaker, and the founder of The Rabbit Room, a non-profit ministry dedicated to fostering spiritual formation and Christ-centered community through story, art, and music. He and Jamie, his wife of twenty-four years, live in a woodsy corner of Nashville they call The Warren.

ALSO BY THE AUTHOR

Books

The Wingfeather Saga

 Book One: On the Edge of the Dark Sea of Darkness

 Book Two: North! Or Be Eaten

 Book Three: The Monster in the Hollows

 Book Four: The Warden and the Wolf King

Wingfeather Tales, ed.

Pembrick's Creaturepedia

The Ballad of Matthew's Begats

Music

Carried Along

Clear to Venus

Love & Thunder

Behold the Lamb of God

The Far Country

Slugs & Bugs & Lullabies (with Randall Goodgame)

Resurrection Letters, Vol. 2

Counting Stars

Above These City Lights

Light for the Lost Boy

After All These Years: A Collection

The Burning Edge of Dawn

Resurrection Letters: Prologue

Resurrection Letters, Vol. 1

—*The*—
RABBIT ROOM

Art Nourishes Community.
Community Nourishes Art.

The Rabbit Room (est. 2006) is a 501(c)3 non-profit
organization that fosters Christ-centered community
and spiritual formation through story, music, and art.

For more information visit
www.RabbitRoom.com.

MUSIC AVAILABLE FROM ANDREW PETERSON

BEHOLD THE LAMB OF GOD

A brand new recording of the album that launched a twenty-year Christmas tour, *Behold the Lamb of God* is a one-of-a-kind album, using Peterson's original Americana-folk sensibilities to tell the story of Jesus' birth as it's prophesied in the Old Testament and brought to bear in the New. Featuring fan favorites such as "Labor of Love," "Matthew's Begats," and more.

RESURRECTION LETTERS

Three albums made over the course of ten years, Andrew Peterson's critically acclaimed *Resurrection Letters: Prologue, Volume I,* and *Volume 2* reflect on the Lent and Easter seasons, professing the weight of Christ's crucifixion and proclaiming the most glorious victory: His defeat of death and our resulting everlasting salvation. Featuring the worship anthem "Is He Worthy?" and more.

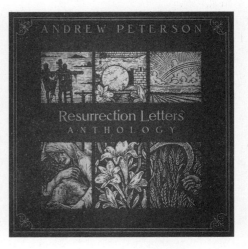